D1189405

WITHDRAWN

THEORIES OF LITERARY REALISM

SUNY Series, The Margins of Literature

Mihai I. Spariosu, Editor

form of a merchandise credit or a merchandise exchange.

Returns without an original receipt will be credited for the current selling price on the date of return, in the form of a merchandise credit or a merchandise exchange. Merchandise deemed final sale on the date of return may not be returned or exchanged.

Returns with gift receipts or exchange receipts for merchandise within 60 days of the transaction date will be credited for the price indicated on the receipt in the form of a merchandise credit or a merchandise exchange. Merchandise returned more than 60 days after the transaction date will be credited for the current selling price.

Final sale merchandise (merchandise with .88 cent price endings) may not be returned or exchanged.

Merchandise Credits: Valid photo identification must be presented to receive or redeem a merchandise credit.

For online returns, please visit LOFTonline.com for complete details on our online return policy. Only merchandise purchased at LOFT stores or LOFTonline.com may be returned to a LOFT store.

One price adjustment on full-priced merchandise may be made within 7 days from the original date of purchase. To receive an adjustment you must present your original receipt.

Returned checks are subject to a service charge of $25 or the maximum allowed by law. The allowable fee for checks returned for insufficient or uncollected funds, together with charges, may be debited electronically from your account using a bank draft drawn from your account.

Gift card terms and conditions apply to the use of Ann Taylor and LOFT gift cards. Please refer to the back of the gift card for all applicable terms and conditions or consult a sales associate.

OUR RETURN PRACTICE

We will gladly accept your return of unwashed and unworn merchandise under the following conditions:

Returns accompanied by the original receipt within 60 days of purchase will be credited for the price paid either in the original form of payment or a merchandise exchange.

Returns accompanied by an original receipt made more than 60 days after the date of purchase will be credited for the current selling price either in the form of a merchandise credit or a merchandise exchange.

008783009620020122201O

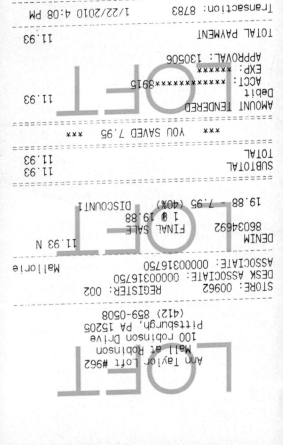

Ann Taylor Loft #962
Mall at Robinson
100 Robinson Drive
Pittsburgh, PA 15205
(412) 859-0508

STORE: 00962   REGISTER: 002
DESK ASSOCIATE: 0000031675O
ASSOCIATE: 0000031675O   Mallorie

DENIM   11.93 N
8603469Z   FINAL SALE
          1 @ 19.88
19.88 - 7.95 (40%) DISCOUNT1

SUBTOTAL   11.93
TOTAL   11.93

===================================
***   YOU SAVED 7.95   ***
===================================

AMOUNT TENDERED   11.93
Debit
ACCT: xxxxxxxxxxxx8915
EXP: xxxxxx
APPROVAL: 130506

TOTAL PAYMENT   11.93

Transaction: 8783   1/22/2010 4:08 PM

Start earning STYLE REWARDS today.
Ask an associate to find out how
or visit STYLEREWARDS.com.

THEORIES OF LITERARY REALISM

DARÍO VILLANUEVA

∾ᴄ∾

TRANSLATED BY
MIHAI I. SPARIOSU AND
SANTIAGO GARCÍA-CASTAÑÓN

REVISED, WITH A NEW PREFACE, BY THE AUTHOR

STATE UNIVERSITY OF NEW YORK PRESS

This book was published in Spain by Espasa-Calpe and Instituto de España, Madrid 1992.

The translation of this book was made possible by a grant from the Dirección General del Libro, Archivos y Bibliotecas of the Spanish Ministry of Education and Culture.

Published by
State University of New York Press, Albany

For information, address State University of New York Press, State University Plaza, Albany, N.Y. 12246

Production by M. R. Mulholland
Marketing by Fran Keneston

Library of Congress Cataloging-in-Publication Data

Villanueva, Darío.
    [Teorías del realismo literario. English]
    Theories of literary realism / Darío Villanueva ; translated by
Mihai I. Spariosu and Santiago Garcia Castanon.
       p.   cm. — (SUNY series, the margins of literature)
    --Rev., with a new pref./by the author.
    Given as a cycle of five lectures at the Instituto de España, in
Madrid, Apr. 1991.
    Includes bibliographical references and index.
    ISBN 0-7914-3327-7 (hc : alk. paper). — ISBN 0-7914-3328-5 (pbk.
: alk. paper)
    1. Realism in literature. I. Title. II. Series.
PN56.R3V5513 1997
809'.912—dc20
                                                96-23293
                                                  CIP

10   9   8   7   6   5   4   3   2   1   **Rev**

I must confess that I cannot understand why our scholars assume an anti-realist stance in academia and a commonsensical (and, therefore, realist) one in everyday life. Being the realist that I am, I recognize this strange fact of academic life and pity those who take anti-realism seriously.

—Mario Bunge, *Racionalidad y realismo*

What is now proved was once only imagined.

—William Blake, *The Prophetic Book*

CONTENTS

PREFACE

Realism has not only shaped important schools and peri-
ods in literary history, but also been a fundamental constant of
all literature, its first theoretical formulation being the principle of *mimesis* in Aristotle's *Poetics*. In this sense, realism
can be regarded as one of the central questions of literary theory, the task of which should be to define the boundaries of
this concept clearly and do away with the imprecision, ambiguity, and polysemia that have often accompanied its use.
This is no easy task, however, for realism involves far-ranging
issues. The first one is of a philosophical nature: what is reality? This question leads to a second, properly aesthetic one:
how can reality be recreated artistically? In turn, this aesthetic
question, when applied specifically to literature, engenders
linguistic problems, such as that of the relation between words
and objects.

The present book deals with the possibilities and limits of
a concept of realism that seeks a point of equilibrium between
the principle of the autonomy of the literary work vis-à-vis
reality and the complex relations that the work clearly establishes with this reality. It acknowledges from the very beginning, then, that it is a personal response to the poststructural-
ist crisis in literary theory. By concentrating on the study of
the literary work of art as a verbal construction, the great
Continental and Anglo-American tradition of formalism and
New Criticism has ended up neglecting the second, mimetic
aspect of the literary problematic and thus dissociating literature from life. In fact, the absence of an equilibrium between
the formal and the mimetic aspects of the literary phenomenon engenders two fallacies that can be called *formal* and
genetic, respectively. One can, however, adopt a third theoretical position: a phenomenology and pragmatics of realism
from the reader's perspective. In this sense, the present work

inscribes itself in the horizon of the Husserlian-Ingardian phenomenology of literature, the German *Rezeptionsaesthetik*,
the Anglo-Saxon reader-response criticism, and, generally, the
recent pragmatic developments in semiotics.

Eight years ago, just as I had completed an early version of
this book, I happened to come across an essay-review of Jürgen
Habermas's *Der philosophische Diskurs der Moderne* (1987)
by Ignacio Sotelo, professor of political science at the Free
University of Berlin, which encouraged me to proceed with a
project that at the time had seemed rather overwhelming.
Now that an English translation of my book is about to come
out, I see in that fortuitous reading encounter an emblematic
premonition of the trajectory of this project. In his essay,
Sotelo contrasts the Napoleonic model of a university with
its German counterpart. Whereas the former is mostly
designed to convey knowledge that has already been acquired,
the latter is largely geared toward new ways of acquiring it, so
that its courses of study are not so much general surveys as
intellectual ventures along the slippery path of a controversial
or unusual topic. According to Sotelo, in the amphitheaters of
the German university teachers primarily present their
thought in progress, debating it with their students and colleagues and leaving its rigorous elaboration to future studies
that are, in turn, inspired from their teaching practice.

The genesis of this book follows Sotelo's second academic
model. The subject of literary realism is, by all accounts,
excessive, but when I took it up in 1986 I felt that even though
it was a fundamental question of literary theory, our standard
approaches to it were not entirely satisfactory; so I devoted a
graduate seminar to it in order to find a way out of my per-
plexities by confronting them in a classroom situation. The
next step was much riskier, as I presented my views on realism in the formal setting of a competition for the first chair in
literary theory at the University of Santiago de Compostela,
submitting them to the judicious critical refutations of five
teachers and colleagues, Fernando Lázaro Carreter, María del
Carmen Bobes Naves, Ricardo Senabre, Jenaro Taléns, and
Miguel Ángel Garrido Gallardo, to whom I remain forever
indebted. Guided by their critical observations, I proceeded to

teach another advanced seminar on literary realism and then asked several friends and colleagues to read a second draft of what I thought at the time to be the final version of this book. One of them, Anxo Tarrío, was generous enough to cite it, even at that early stage, in his excellent study of Álvaro Cunqueiro, a writer who makes the labyrinth of realism even more complicated, if that is possible. Finally, Miguel Artola invited me to give a cycle of five lectures on literary realism at the Instituto de España in Madrid, thereby closing the prophetic circle that I saw in Sotelo's German academic model of acquiring knowledge. So in April 1991, I had a last chance of testing my ideas against a live audience, and this renewed dialogue with a select group of colleagues and friends, including such prominent writers as the much-regretted Elena Quiroga (who left us in October 1995), led me to revising my "work in progress" once again. The five lectures at the Instituto de España became the five chapters of the present book, to which I put the finishing touches in December 1991, five years after its conception.

The publication of *Teorías del realismo literario* in the spring of 1992 did not pass unnoticed in Spain, coinciding with a heated public debate around the alleged rejection of contemporary Spanish realist painting by the directors of the Reina Sofía Museum in Madrid. This fortuitous circumstance probably favored the wide circulation of my book despite its decidedly academic, rather than essayistic, character. It must also account for the fact that it was among the five finalists for the essay category of the *Premio Nacional de Literatura* offered by the Spanish Ministry of Culture, to which I am also greatly indebted for its generous support in arranging for this work to be translated into English.

Since then, the renewed theoretical interest in realism has not faded, but rather increased, as witnessed not only by the various Spanish and foreign reviews of *Teorías del realismo* but, above all, by the publication of several other books on this topic. Among them stand out the collective volume on *Realism and Representation* edited by George Levin (1992) and the one on *Realism* edited by Lilian Furst (1992), as well as Wolfgang Iser's *The Fictive and the Imaginary* (1993),

Umberto Eco's *Six Walks in the Fictional Woods* (1994), and
Henri Mitterand's *L'illusion réaliste* (1994). In Spain I should
also mention J. D. Pujante Sánchez's *Mimesis y siglo XX*
(1992), T. M. Albaladejo's *Semántica de la narración: la ficción
realista* (1992), J. M. Pozuelo Yvancos's *Poética de la ficción*
(1993), as well as the collective volume on *Ficcionalidad y
escritura*, edited by V. J. Benet and M. L. Bruguera (1994).
Pozuelo Yvancos's study is especially close to mine, as both of
us share the premise that the theoretical problem of literary
fictionality can be approached less from a semantic than from
an essentially pragmatic perspective, pragmatics being the part
of semantics that deals with the relation between signs and
their users, in our particular case, the relation between literary
authors and their readers.

Of course, there are occult ways of denying the importance of literary pragmatics as a mediator between formalist
immanentism and the view of literature as an active historical
and social institution that transcends the purely aesthetic
realm. For example, Tomás Albaladejo's study promotes the
idea of a so-called "extensional semantics," which, judging
from the attribute "extensional," wishes to ground itself
exclusively in a referential realm that is empirical and, therefore, external to the literary text. By contrast, I believe that the
entire field of literary semantics should develop within the
strict limits of the text. At the same time that the literary
work textually creates its own internal referential world, however, it also establishes, through its readers, a dialogue with
the real world, with the external field of reference that each
reader brings to the text.

What can be more pragmatic than such a dialogue? So
the problem of fictionality and, therefore, that of realism can
best be approached from the standpoint of pragmatics, to
which Charles Peirce contributed so much. This is what
Siegfried Schmidt proposed in 1976, followed by Paul Ricoeur
who, in *Temps et récit I* (his opus magnum, begun in 1983),
speaks of an *intersection* between the world of the text and the
world of the auditor or reader. Ricoeur is the first to distinguish among three different aspects of Aristotelian *mimesis* as
generating the entire dialectics between the work, its creator,

and its reader: *mimesis I*, involving a pre-compositional stage; *mimesis II*, or *mimesis*-creation, resulting in the work proper; and finally *mimesis III*, which, far from simply reproducing the real, is a dynamic, creative activity that originates primarily in the relation between the text and the reader who actualizes and recreates it. My own theoretical objective over the years has been to situate literary realism precisely within this third perspective.

I have also greatly benefited from the reviews of *Teorías del realismo*, of which I can mention only two in the present context: one by Fernando Lázaro Carreter, the dean of contemporary Spanish literary theory (in the June 1992 issue of the *ABC Cultural*—the Spanish equivalent of the *Times Literary Supplement*); and the other by Francisco Ayala, one of the greatest Spanish novelists of this century as well as a distingushed literary critic (in the December 1992 issue of *Saber Leer*—a review that Ayala calls precisely "El realismo literario"). Among their many perceptive comments, I have especially taken to heart Lázaro Carreter's suggestion that I should, in the near future, supplement my primarily theoretical book with an analytical, diachronic study of how the successive systems of realist creations have perpetuated a literary realism through which we, the readers, associate the fictional universe generated by the literary form with our own real-life experiences on both an individual and a social level.

As to Francisco Ayala, in addition to his insightful "Literary Realism" and his illuminating essays on the great Spanish realists, including Benito Pérez Galdós, I should like to mention his wonderful example of what I call "intentional realism," included in his memoirs, *Recuerdos y olvidos* (Madrid, Alianza Editorial, 1988, 425), à propos of his novel, *Muertes de perro* (which he wrote in the United States in the wake of his earlier exile in Buenos Aires and Puerto Rico, and which was first published in 1958). This novel is a satirical portrait of a political dictatorship, which the author places in an imaginary Central American republic in order to free himself from a rigid historical referent and incorporate material from various literary models in the Hispanic tradition of Valle-Inclán and Miguel Ángel Asturias, subsequently taken up not only by Ayala, but also by Augusto Roa Bastos and Gabriel García Márquez, among others. Despite this obvious literary device, Ayala recalls that a journalist from Nicaragua (a country the novelist had never visited) approached him at the end of one of his New York lectures and surprised him by exclaiming: "But, how well you know my country! I've had no trouble guessing the real name of every character in your novel."

The long and laborious process that has preceded the present English version of *Teorías del realismo* is certainly no guarantee of its future success, yet I believe that it is very useful not only to weave and unweave our own theoretical conjectures, but also to submit them periodically to successive tests of verification and possible refutation. Under the shrewd scrutiny of my generous critics, I have already discarded several ideas that had at one time seemed solid and trustworthy. I have no doubt, however, that the most stringent test is yet to come, now that SUNY Press plans to include my book in Mihai I. Spariosu's "The Margins of Literature" series—for which I am very grateful—and thus to make it available to other readers, who will be no less severe and perspicatious than the earlier ones and before whom, moreover, I cannot defend my theoretical adventures in person and in my own language. Although a frequent visitor and lecturer at various North American universities, as well as an editor, together with Silvia L. López and Jenaro Taléns, of a recent North American volume, *Critical Practices in Post-Franco Spain* (Minneapolis and London: University of Minnesota Press, 1994), I certainly do not discount the possibility that certain aspects of the present book may appear alien or obscure to my new addressees. But it would go against my own theoretical propositions not to trust in their vigorous, productive response, for which I would like to thank them in advance. Finally, I would also like to thank Mihai I. Spariosu and Santiago García-Castañón for performing on my text the generous reading and rewriting operation that we call translation.

1

GENETIC REALISM

It may seem superfluous to address the question of realism once again, in view of the fact that since the mid-nineteenth century it has in all likelihood been the single most debated topic among literary scholars and artists alike. And yet, this question is perhaps worth revisiting because its far-reaching scope, the large number of possible answers to it, and the contradictory nature of many of these answers—due in part to the polemical tone that has always accompanied the discussion on realism—require a continuous revision of previous conclusions. And all the more so when some of these conclusions suffer—as I have just implied—not only from ambiguities but also from a troubling polysemia that blurs the boundaries of the concept.

Echoing these problems in the wake of, among others, Benedetto Croce and Karl Mannheim, Harry Levin cites, in one of his fundamental books about realism (1974, 87–89), George Moore's somewhat hyperbolic, and for that very reason extremely eloquent, statement, highlighting the far-reaching range of the concept: "There has never been a literary school other than realism." Moore's statement implies that the question of realism goes beyond the scope of a certain literary period or trend, such as the nineteenth-century French and other European schools and their successors up to the present, precisely because it is a constant of all literature (as well as of all other arts).

If the first, historical aspect of realism falls within the purview of literary history, criticism, and comparative studies as disciplines belonging to the science of literature, the second, conceptual aspect falls entirely within the scope of literary theory, which could well make it the main focus of its interest, in the manner in which Aristotle grounded his *Poetics* in the principle of *mimesis*. In fact, *mimesis* was the classical name of the relationship between literature and reality before it was replaced by the relatively recent term "realism."

A retrospective glance at the numerous past explorations of literary realism reveals that many of the difficulties that we presently encounter in rethinking the topic have perhaps derived from a confusion of its three different facets: realism as a period or school in modern and contemporary literature; realism as a constant feature of all of these schools as well as of their precursors; and lastly, realism as an object of theoretical reflection.

Historical contributions, such as the one by Harry Levin (1974) or the equally familiar one by René Wellek (1961), are the most frequent, and they are certainly necessary, as are the critical studies of a stylistic nature, among which Auerbach's *Mimesis* (1942) stands out. But, by virtue of the necessary interdependence of all the basic disciplines comprising the science of literature, one cannot ignore the purely theoretical aspect that should enable us to define the concepts of realism and mimesis in an unambiguous manner. It is true that such theoretical concepts can be reached only by starting from identifiable common elements in concrete texts and literary series; but one cannot chronicle or critically evaluate realistic literature in the absence of a clear theoretical formulation.

We do not lack historical examples of the cavalier way in which the definition of the concept as well as the theoretical framework of literary realism has been treated. Reviewing Auerbach's book in 1954, René Wellek (1954, 304–305) blamed him precisely for his "extreme reluctance to define his terms and to make his suppositions clear from the outset," a flaw resulting from the false belief that a textual analysis with certain historical implications such as Auerbach's could succeed "without a clear theoretical framework." (Recently, Christopher Prendergast [1986, 212] has reiterated the same judgment: "Auerbach's magisterial *Mimesis* is magisterial precisely because for him the concept of 'mimesis' as such was intrinsically non problematic.") According to E. B. Greenwood

(1962, 89), Wellek himself committed a similar error when seven years later, perhaps stimulated by his dissatisfaction with Auerbach's book, he devoted a critical study to "The Concept of Realism in Literary Scholarship" (Wellek 1961), separating, in Greenwood's words, "the period realism from the perennial realism," ignoring "the fundamental epistemological problem of the relation of art and reality"—that is, the most genuinely theoretical aspect of the realistic-mimetic question—and confining himself to a definition of realism as "the objective representation of the current social reality."

There is also Anna Seghers's interesting request in an epistolary exchange with Georg Lukács between 1938 and 1939 (collected in the latter's *Probleme der Realismus*, 1955, 323–329): "Please define once again what you mean exactly by realism. This request is not gratuitous. In your discussion, all terminology is employed in a very different, and occasionally imprecise way" (Letter of June 28, 1938). Neither would Lukács's response satisfy his correspondent: "To me your letter was nothing but a partial answer" (February 1939). Thus, the old vices that Roman Jakobson had denounced around 1921 in his essay on artistic realism were very much alive in the late thirties (and to some extent still are). Jakobson attributed the inoperativity of the concept to the vague and empty verbiage with which literary research attempted to define it as the artistic trend leaning toward reproducing reality as faithfully as possible and aiming at a maximum of verisimilitude; to the absolute relativism with which the realistic criterion was applied to both innovative and traditional writers; and to the tautological frivolity of conferring this attribute upon certain literatures as a defining feature, in the same way in which one could aphoristically proclaim that "the twenties are an age proper to man" (Jakobson 1921, 98–108).

Precisely this last type of tautological argument, applied to Spanish literature, had provoked a vigorous reaction from Ortega y Gasset in 1912, whose challenge to young scholars to enter the lists in favor of dismantling the false notion identifying Spanish literature with realism was seconded by Dámaso Alonso in his well-known essay "Escila y Caribdis," published in 1927. Years later, Ramón Menéndez Pidal considered the term "extremely imprecise," a phrase that serves as a motto for a study by Fernando Lázaro Carreter, published in 1969 in homage to his by then deceased master and entitled "El realismo como concepto crítico-literario." In this study, Lázaro Carreter asserts that realism "has been given such diverse hues and has been carved with so many faces . . . that by meaning so much it has come to mean almost nothing" (Lázaro Carreter 1969, 125). A few years before Lázaro Carreter, Stefan Morawski (1963, 52) had also denounced its polysemic ambiguity, and a year after, Damian Grant, in a respectable monograph (1970, 1), ventured to call it the most elastic and prodigious of literary terms, suffering from a chronic instability evident from its tendency to accumulate adjectives, of which he listed no less than two dozen.

I share many of Lázaro Carreter's general assumptions and conclusions in the present book, which I see as a continuation of his study as well as a further contribution to a difficult and important debate—a debate that has already provoked wide discussions outside of Spain without having much of an echo among us, so that Carreter could reasonably claim that he attempted to "break the silence, or, if one wishes, to rekindle the flame" (1969, 121). Indeed, although Spanish writers and what Northrop Frye liked to call "public critics" did carry out a debate in the sixties about novelistic realism and neorealism—social, critical, and so forth—one can find nothing of interest in this regard in the Spanish scholarly world, with the exception of a timid attempt, closely related to Lázaro Carreter's study (cf. Alfonso Rey Álvarez 1970, and Lázaro Carreter 1970). In those days, the very evolution of literary theory (and even that of Spanish narrative and poetic genres), influenced by a formalist approach, as well as the pendular reaction against a very strict poetics identified with formalism, doubly favored the lack of critical interest in realism (and not only in Spain; in Italy, for example, Piero Raffa—1967, 272—discerned in many of his country's artists and intellectuals a deliberate tendency of avoiding the topic or even the term).

For all these reasons, therefore, it does not seem inappropriate to confront the issue of realism again today. Although the difficulties in tackling this issue have not gone away, I trust that the development of our disciplines in the last two decades will provide us with a critical-theoretical methodology, if not completely new, at least partially modified. In any case, I shall attempt to reexamine the fundamental principle of literary realism from the perspective of contemporary discourse theory, just as Raffa examined it in the sixties from the perspective of a semiology of art, which was then in vogue in Italy and France, but was still far from reaching Spain.

Realism and Mimesis

Raffa himself (1967, 280–281) states that realism understood as a faithful and non-distorted aesthetic reproduction of external phenomena as we perceive them "can be considered a particular version of the old principle of mimesis," because in the end it represents the continuation of that perennial literary constant by which the art of discourse has never ceased to relate to human and physical reality, albeit in a rather complex and subtle manner, engendering numerous theoretical puzzles. A confusion between the theoretical and historical levels is precisely what caused Jan Bruck (1982, 190) to maintain paradoxically that Aristotelian *mimesis* "has nothing to do with 'realism,'" for the former is a "general characteristic of all works of art and literature" whereas the latter is a particular mode of representation confined to a certain epoch or school. The scholarly consensus actually runs the opposite way. The very title of Auerbach's book (*Mimesis: The Representation of Reality in Western Literature*) assumes the common identity of mimesis and realism, and one of the most rigorous contributions to the subject, Stephan Kohl's *Realismus: Theorie und Geschichte* (1977), establishes a firm line of continuity between classical mimesis and modern realism, from Plato to the "nouveau roman." M. H. Abrams, in his book on Romantic aesthetics and the critical tradition (1953), also emphasizes the mimetic constant throughout the history of literature.

But what is perhaps of even greater relevance is the first nineteenth-century realists' acknowledgement of the close kinship between their postulates and those of Platonic-

Aristotelian *mimesis*. George J. Becker's very useful collection of documents on modern literary realism (1963) abounds in such acknowledgments. For example, Louis Edouard Duranty, in his journal called precisely *Réalisme* (published during 1856 and 1857, in the aftermath of the furor that Gustave Courbet's painting exhibit and realist manifesto produced in Paris), stated that the new artistic procedure had always existed and that the only new thing about it was its name (Becker 1963, 97). Around the same time, *The Westminster Review*, which had first introduced the term in English in 1853 with an article on Balzac, published another piece in which G. H. Lewes defined the new school in the same terms that had been used by Aristotle in relation to *mimesis* (Becker 1963, 6). One should, moreover, note that Lewes, when translating the term *mimesis*, prefers at times to use "representation" instead of "imitation," as some of the most recent translators of the *Poetics* do (cf. Mieke Bal, 1982. Also V. Bozal, 1987, and M. I. Spariosu—editor—1984).

Although the modern literary term originates in Aristotle, the real roots of *mimesis* go back to Plato's thought, where it transcends a strictly artistic context, being at the core of his entire idealistic philosophy. This is one more indication of the enormous complexity of the problem of realism, for, apart from the various literary perspectives one can bring to it, there are at least three fundamental aspects of it that will necessarily concern us in the present study. The first is, of course, the philosophical aspect. The very denomination of "realism" has its origins in the old dispute about the universals or archetypal ideas to which Plato granted absolute reality. Consequently, as Book Ten of the *Republic* indicates, for Plato poetic imitation appears to be conditioned by what W. J. Verdenius (1949, 16) calls "his conception of a hierarchical structure of reality." Plato thus presupposes three levels of reality: that of the ideal or archetypal forms, whose ontological validity cannot be questioned; that of the visible objects or phenomena, which are nothing but pale reflections of ideal forms; and a third level composed of images, which would comprise the mimetic arts in general and literature in particular; and these usually take as a model a sensible reality which in turn is an imperfect copy of a more genuine one. Therefore, a direct literary imitation is located two steps below the essential nature of things, and a truly ambitious art of realism must rise above the always precarious material world in order to approach ideal reality, different from its visual appearance.

Aristotle departs radically from this paradoxical Platonic identification of realism with idealism, as well as from a concept of *mimesis* which refers to the basic relationship between the archetypal (*paradeigmatos eidos*) and the sensible-perceptible (*mimema paradeigmatos*) and which, therefore, goes well beyond the restricted realm of art. Without rejecting the concept of universals, Aristotle does not consider the latter alien to things but, rather, incarnated in and derivable only from them. That is why Mario Bunge (1985, 42) warns of the absurdity of speaking only of *philosophical realism*, for one has to acknowledge from the beginning, as a result of this Platonic-Aristotelian confrontation, a *metaphysical realism* as opposed to a gnoseological one.

The first consequence of this second, Aristotelian realism is that sensible reality does not appear to be an image of anything that transcends it, and that *mimesis* definitely confines itself to the specific realm of art and literature. In this respect, Richard McKeon (1936, 161–162) notes in a major study on literary criticism and the concept of imitation in classical Antiquity: "For Aristotle imitation is not, at one extreme, the imitation of ideas, such as philosophers and the Demiurge indulge in according to Plato. . . . Moreover, for Aristotle imitation is not an imitation of an idea in the mind of the artist; . . . imitation is of particular things; the object of imitation, according to the statement of the *Poetics* . . . is the actions of men." Therefore, as M. H. Abrams (1953, 25) also emphasizes, in Aristotle the word *mimesis* becomes a specific term for the arts "that distinguishes them from everything else in the Universe, liberating them from competition with other human activities" (Abrams 1953, 25; cf. also Boyd 1968, 133). Going against the strictly mimetic principle of the Platonic concept, Aristotle identifies it with a *representation* of reality.

There is a very obvious kinship, then, between the general ontological, epistemological, and philosophical principles of what Jan Bruck (1982) calls eighteenth- and nineteenth-century "bourgeois" realism (which, as I have already pointed out, Bruck wishes to see as something alien and different from Aristotelian *mimesis*) and Aristotle's concept of art and reality. As a matter of fact, the tradition of rationalism, sensualism, and empiricism—starting with Descartes, Locke, and Berkeley, continuing with Thomas Reid's school of "common sense," and going all the way to nineteenth-century positivism—does not constitute, in this regard, any substantial break with Aristotelian philosophy, for it tends to strengthen the reality of the objects perceptible in themselves, outside the perceiving mind. It is not surprising, therefore, that Ian Watt, in his book on the consolidation of the realistic novel in eighteenth- and nineteenth-century English literature, should state that "this literary change was analogous to the rejection of universals and the emphasis on particulars which characterizes philosophic realism. Aristotle might have agreed with Locke's primary assumption [in *Essay Concerning Human Understanding*, Bk. 1, Ch. 2, sect. XV], that it was the senses which 'at first let in particular ideas, and fournish the empty cabinet' of the mind" (1957, 15).

Quite different, however, are the aesthetic consequences of a particular conception of reality and the world, as noted by Max Wundt (Ermatinger 1930, 427–452). So, for example, an artist steeped in Platonism will be a *realist* through the stylized forms, purified from the world of the senses, liberating this world from its imperfections and bringing it closer to the archetypes; whereas an Aristotelian artist will present the visible in an integrative manner, in order to discover an authentic reality in it. That is the distance separating a pastoral novel such as *Diana* from *Lazarillo de Tormes*, or the treatment of a mythological theme by a Renaissance painter, such as Boticcelli, from the treatment of the same theme by a Baroque artist, such as Velázquez or Rubens.

Therefore, the philosophical component determines the artistic component, and the second fundamental implication of realism and mimesis is precisely an aesthetic one. Some often-quoted definitions of realism consider both components, such as Becker's in his *Documents of Modern Literary*

Realism (1963, 36): "Realism, then, is a formula of art which, conceiving of reality in a certain way, undertakes to present a simulacrum of it on the basis of more or less fixed rules." Becker's discreet caveat concerning the different manners in which the writers who consider themselves realists conceive of the world is expressed in a much stronger form by Raffa (1967, 316) when he warns that "a theory of realism, if it truly wants to escape the limitations of a particular poetics, cannot or should not offer any specific definition of reality."

Consequently, there are different poetics, various formulas and artistic rules that will produce realism, so that, as I have argued from the beginning, I will not identify realism with any specific school or trend, not even with the one that specifically bears its name in the nineteenth century, but rather with this other mimetic constant of art that beholds and reproduces reality creatively. In this regard, one can mention a second aesthetic aspect, proposed by Fernando Lázaro Carreter in the form of a central conclusion of his study: "literary realism is a phenomenon that takes place within a literary series as its dynamic principle, i.e., as an ideal which guides the artists in their quest for novelty, and which always subjects itself to the law of estrangement [in the Russian formalist sense of the term]. This estrangement is one of the multiple conventions that make literature possible and may include a search for unusual angles of observation, a presentation of rare realities—the more "real," the more verifiable—and, of course, an interposition of stylistic variations. The 'ingenuous' perspectives and plain language can effect a high degree of estrangement in contrast to prevailing procedures, if the latter are based upon a clear exhibition of artifice" (1969, 141).

But, in addition to the philosophical and the purely aesthetic aspects, there is a third aspect that largely conditions the theoretical understanding of realism, namely language.

Mimesis and Language

In *The Mirror and the Lamp*, M. H. Abrams shows how from the time of the full rediscovery of Aristotle in the Italian cinquecento until the mid-eighteenth century, the principle of *mimesis* had generally been accepted as a foundation of all art, according to the text of the first chapter of the *Poetics* (1447a 10–21), which does not speak only of what we moderns understand by literature. Thus, Aristotle says:

> Epic poetry and Tragedy, Comedy also and Dithyrambic poetry, and the music of the flute and of the lyre most of their forms, are all in their general conception modes of imitation. They differ, however, from one another in three respects,—the medium, the objects, the manner or mode of imitation, being in each case distinct.
>
> For as there are persons who, by conscious art or mere habit, imitate and represent various objects through the medium of color and form, or again by the voice; so in the arts above mentioned, taken as a whole, the imitation is produced by rhythm, language, or "harmony," either singly or combined.
>
> Thus in the music of the flute and of the lyre, "harmony" and rhythm alone are employed; also in other arts, such as that of the shepherd's pipe, which are essentially similar to these. In dancing, rhythm alone is used without "harmony"; for even dancing imitates character, emotion, and action, by rhythmical movement. (tr. S. H. Butcher 1907, 7–8)

But Abrams also points out that in the eighteenth century there were several Aristotelian commentators who paid close attention to the different means of imitation employed by various arts. Consequently, whereas in 1744 James Harris still stated in a "Discourse on Music, Painting and Poesie" that *mimesis* was common to the three arts despite the instrumental differences between them, some years later, Henry Home, Lord Kames, restricted that principle to painting and sculpture. According to him, music and architecture were no longer a "copy of nature," but "productive of originals"; and literature, of which language is the medium of expression, could be considered mimetic only when imitating the sounds and movement of reality.

In 1789, Thomas Twining, also a translator and commentator of the *Poetics*, went even further. Anticipating the modern findings of Saussurean linguistics and Morris's semiotics, Twining proposed that the iconic arts (those that are similar to what they denote) be distingushed from those that signify by mere convention. Hence, pure *mimesis* should be reserved for the arts whose forms display an immediate and obvious likeness to the copied model; namely, painting, sculpture, and drawing. Music is not imitative in any way, and of literature only the dramatic can be considered as such, for it imitates speech with speech, bodies with bodies, light with light, sound with sound, etc. (Abrams 1953, 31–32).

So the problematic of the medium of imitation within the Aristotelian tradition introduces the third basic aspect of the theoretical concept of realism, i.e., the linguistic one. The fundamental importance of this aspect hardly needs to be emphasized, as it points to the very core of literature as a verbal art, so that sooner or later one must always come back to it. The fact that words are, with a few exceptions, purely symbolic rather than iconic signs, and that their ability to signify has no direct relation to what they signify is no sufficient reason to deny the mimetic potential of all the non-dramatic genres; it nevertheless introduces a large number of new elements that cannot be ignored, considerably complicating the process of the mimetic representation of reality that the verbal art *de facto* involves.

Today, we have certainly moved far away from the empirical theory of language in Locke's *Essay Concerning Human Understanding* (1690), according to which words are direct images of reality, of things perceived through the senses, even though Locke's linguistic ideas have remained substantially unchanged until as recently as the early Wittgenstein (1921), for whom language represents a sort of scale map of the whole world. As we read in *Tractatus Logico-Philosophicus* (5–6), "die Grenzen meiner Sprache bedeuten die Grenzen meiner Welt" ("the limits of my language mean the limits of my world," 1921, 163). Wittgenstein's early concept of language, no less than Locke's, ultimately suffers from the same "referential fallacy" that Umberto Eco (1975) mentions in his well-known treatise on semiotics.

The distance between a literary realism based on Platonic thought and one based on Aristotelian principles has thus been duplicated by the distance between a linguistic *mimesis* of the Lockean kind and the other linguistic view that discards the idea of words as transparent images, granting them the full power of creating, by themselves, the world of which they speak to us; words have this power because of their inner efficiency and their combinatory skill as "language games," in the manner of the later Wittgenstein, for whom there are no essential meanings anymore, but only relative ones. All of the issues pertaining to language, including that of its relation to reality, have now become one of the main concerns—if not the primary concern—of contemporary philosophy, both in the so-called analytic schools and in the neopositivistic ones.

In sum, the linguistic, aesthetic, and philosophical implications of realism are so numerous that it is almost impossible to deal with all of them in a single study, which would, moreover, have to stray far beyond the realm of literary theory. Nevertheless, I wish to address a specific issue within this vast problematic, in which various philosophical, aesthetic, and linguistic elements come together, namely the apparent contradiction between two basic assumptions that are equally important for a correct understanding of the literary phenomenon and yet seem at first sight to exclude each other. I am referring, on the one hand, to the principle of the autonomy of the literary work and, on the other hand, to the remarkable relation of the literary work to reality—a relation without which literature could not play the role of an authentic social institution that it undoubtedly plays and would most certainly lose the interest that has motivated readers of all times to turn to it again and again.

One of the necessary requirements for understanding in depth the working of a literary text is to consider it in a strictly immanent fashion, according to the fruitful and indispensible legacy of the various formalisms that have marked the development of literary criticism and theory in our century. The verbal work of art is ruled by its own laws, and what affirms its essence as such, its *literariness*, has nothing to do with the referential matter that it may convey to us, but

purely with the articulation of its forms, i.e., with its composition and style. But along with this centripetal drive by which
literature gives us an account of its own essential being, the
formalists themselves acknowledge, as René Wellek (a staunch
defender, since the nineteen forties, of the "intrinsic access" to
the work of art) recently indicates, that "literature does refer to
reality, says something about the world, and makes us see and
know the external world and that of our own and other
minds" (Wellek 1982, 30).

It is true that today one need no longer rethink the point
of equilibrium between literature and reality, although a not
too distant past forced upon the student of literature an
unequivocal choice between the notion of autonomous art
and that of art as a witness and reflection of reality. As might
be expected, both positions gave rise to fallacies that can be
called *aesthetic* (or *formal*) and *mimetic* (or *genetic*), respectively; and both of them resulted from a utopian attempt to
explain a phenomenon as complex as literature from a single,
exclusive standpoint, as if it were not possible to work out a
notion of realism on a solid theoretical basis that would transcend such oppositions. As our questions become more complex, so will the conceptual arsenal required for answering
them. In attempting to develop an integrative notion of realism, we need not only constantly to interweave aesthetic, linguistic, and philosophical aspects, but also to evaluate each
and every factor that intervenes in the complex literary
process (i.e., the author, the text, and the reader).

Although my ultimate goal is to reach a balanced understanding of literature as an art form and a sign of reality, I
shall first consider the position—of which Damian Grant's
study (1970) can be a perfect illustration—that assumes not
one, but two critical-literary modes of realism, akin to the
antinomies and the oppositions I have just mentioned. The
first mode places a special emphasis on the literary work's
ability to imitate or reproduce a reality external to it,
whereas the second mode shifts its focus from a world that
precedes the text to another world, autonomously created
within it. This other world results not so much from imitation or correspondence, but from an imaginative creation

that filters the objective materials presumably at the origin of the whole process, subjecting them to a principle of immanent coherence that will make them signify more through an estrangement from, rather than an identification with, factual reality.

In the pages that follow I shall describe these two main theoretical positions that advocate, on the one hand, a "realism of correspondence," also called "conscientious realism" by Grant (1970) and "subject-matter realism" by Göran Sörbom (1966); and, on the other hand, a "realism of coherence," which Grant calls "conscious realism" and Sörbom, "formal realism." Given the basic principle of interdependence among all literary disciplines, I shall certainly resort to concrete textual examples, even though I shall have to limit them severely because of space considerations. The same considerations will play a role in dealing with an issue which I have already mentioned briefly and which also requires a large amount of historical documentation: the conceptual identity and temporal continuity between Aristotelian *mimesis* and modern realism, consecrated in the nineteenth century. Although I cannot explore this issue in detail, I shall frequently refer to the most important past contributions to it, both those focusing on the mimetic principle—for example the work of M. H. Abrams (1953), John D. Boyd (1968), Jan Bruck (1982), Hermann Koller (1954), J. D. Lyons and S. G. Nichols, editors (1982), Richard McKeon (1936), Göran Sörbom (1966), Mihai I. Spariosu, editor (1984), Wladyslaw Tatarkiewicz (1987), J. Tate (1928, 1932), W. F. Trench (1933), and W. J. Verdenius (1949)—and those recording the appearance of the term "realism" in different European languages and the avatars of its technical-literary meaning: E. B. O. Bornecque and P. Cogny (1963), Bernard R. Bowron Jr. (1959), Robert Gorham Davis (1951), H. U. Forest (1926), Henry C. Hatfield (1951), F. W. J. Hemmings, editor (1974), Stephan Kohl (1977), Harry Levin (1963), Renato Poggioli (1951), Wolfgang Preisendanz (1977), Christopher Prendergast (1986), Albert J. Salvan (1951), J. P. Stern (1973), J. L. Styan (1981), A. J. Tieje (1913), Ian Watt (1957), Bernard Weinberg (1937), and René Wellek (1961).

The Concept of Genetic Realism

The first of the two critical-literary modes of realism is based on a principle of transparent correspondence between the literary text and external phenomena (Northrop Frye 1976, 798), being mainly of genetic origin. It has generally tended toward a pure and elemental literalism, and more so in the theoretical-critical descriptions of it than in artistic practice. For, as René Wellek (1961, 223) points out, "in the history of literary criticism the concept of imitation was, whatever its exact meaning in Aristotle may have been, often interpreted as literal copying, as naturalism." Wellek understands "naturalism" as it essentially was: an exacerbation of the postulates of nineteenth-century realism and their articulation in a theoretical system perfectly adjusted to a literary practice that affected a large number of subsequent works as well. This theoretical system, moreover, was clearly linked to the mimetic tradition. For example, reviewing Jane Austen's *Emma* in 1815, Walter Scott defined the novel as the art of copying nature as it is.

Naturalism is nothing but genetic realism, for it assumes the existence of a univocal reality which precedes the text and which is scanned by the author's perceiving consciousness in all its hidden aspects through minute and efficient observation. Its result should be a faithful reproduction of this reality, owing to the transparency or thinness of the literary medium (language) and to the artist's "sincerity." We find this theory of genetic realism structured to the last detail in Zola, although all of its components had already appeared separately throughout the nineteenth century. In "Le roman expérimental," Zola proclaims the starting point that is true reality: "Nous partions bien des fait vrais, qui sont notre base indestructible" (Zola 1971, 66). "Plus de lyrisme," Zola adds in his "Lettre à la jeunesse," "plus des grands mots vides, mais des faits, des documents" (1971, 135). But it is in another essay, "Le naturalisme au thèatre," that Zola introduces the second fundamental factor of genetic realism, the observer, and then links his theory with Aristotle and Boileau—to the latter we owe the well-known lines in *L'Art poétique*: "Rien n'est beau que le vrai: le vrai seul est aimable;/il doit régner partout, et même dans la fable." Zola claims only to "avoir inventé et lancé un mot nouveau, pour désigner une école lit-téraire vieille comme le monde" (1971, 139). Here Zola also inserts his famous definition of fiction as "un coin de la nature vu à travers un tempérament" (1971, 140), with the two basic ingredients of a realist work, nature and the subject that per-ceives it, i.e., a double genetic principle: a) "Le retour à la nature et à l'homme, l'observation directe, l'anatomie exacte, l'acceptation et la peinture de ce qui est" (Zola 1971, 143); and b) "Je suis simplement un observateur qui constate les faits" (1971, 139). In sum, "le sens du réel, c'est de sentir la nature et de la rendre telle qu'elle est" (Zola 1971, 215). Hence Zola's absolute identification of his novelistic job and method with that of an experimental scientist. He propounds geneti-cism because "la nature suffit"; it is only a matter of "l'ac-cepter telle q'elle est, sans la modifier ni la rogner en rien; elle est assez belle, assez grande, pour apporter avec elle un com-mencement, un milieu et un fin" (Zola 1971, 149).

Zola's arguments possess a high theoretical value, sum-ming up most accurately the various ways of understanding mimesis and realism that had immediately preceded him. It is not my intention to outline a history of the theoretical con-ceptualizations of realism, especially since the Polish aes-thetician, Wladyslaw Tatarkiewicz (1987) has already accom-plished this task. So here I shall simply limit myself to giving a few examples of the genetic view.

In Russian literary criticism, for instance, Vissarion Grigorevich Belinsky advocated, in 1835, a modern *realistic* literature in the sense of a faithful reproduction, rather than creation, of life as it is (Becker 1963, 41–43). In turn, Nikolay Gavrilovich Chernishevsky (acknowledged by Marx and Lenin as a quintessential materialist philosopher), in an 1853 essay attempting to apply Feuerbach's philosophy to major aesthetic issues, maintained that the main goal of the art work was to reproduce what occurs in real life and concerns human beings.

During the early 1850s, the term "realism" as such, as well as in the literary sense that concerns us, began to appear in English journals such as *Fraser's Magazine* and *The*

Westminster Review. (Soon afterward, during the same decade, the first occurrences of the adjective *realista* are documented in Spanish. Cf. Fernando Lázaro Carreter 1969, 122, n. 1.) But as early as 1821, in the *Mercure français du XIXe siècle* (XIII, 6), the word, the concept, and its complete identification with *mimesis* became part of the French language through an anonymous article: "Cette doctrine littéraire qui gagne tous les jours du terrain et qui conduirait à une fidèle imitation non pas des chefs-d'oeuvre de l'art mais des originaux que nous offre la nature, pourrait fort bien s'appeller le *réalisme*: ce serait suivant quelques apparences, la littérature dominante du XIXe siècle, la littérature du vrai" (in Elbert B. O. Borgerhoff 1938, 839).

But it is the late 1850s that witness the controvesial irruption of genetic realism as a school or an artistic—mainly literary—movement on the French cultural scene. From there it spreads throughout Europe, with the famous "Pavillon du Réalisme" and Courbet's manifesto, with Duranty's journal *Réalisme* and Champfleury's essay of the same title, and finally with the release of *Madame Bovary*, following a court trial.

Champfleury was a fervent champion of "sincerity" as a root of art; according to that principle, he divided writers into two groups, *sinceristes* and *formalistes*, a division that corresponds to the two modes of realism under consideration here. Needless to say, Champfleury regarded the non-genetic or "formal" realists as the more inconsistent of the two. In fact, in addition to the solid evidence of a univocal and unquestionable reality, the guarantee of an authentic realism of the sincere kind lies in the artist's capacity of observation—but not particularly and exclusively in his artistic abilities—and above all in his faithful compliance with the truth—in his sincerity; this is one of the three necessary requirements for creating an authentic work of art, together with a clear expression and the moral truth of the subject matter, as Tolstoy argued in an 1894 article on Maupassant. According to Abrams (1953, 564), moreover, sincerity "became a favorite Victorian test of literary virtue," as George Henry Lewes and Matthew Arnold demonstrated. In sum, "the realist ideal" means, in Becker's words (1963, 32), "to come as close as possible to observed experience." Such ideas of genetic realism have persisted in both theory and artistic practice up to the present day.

The Goncourt brothers were also loyal champions of genetic realism. For example, in presenting their *Germinie Lacerteux* to the public in 1864, they categorically stated: "Le public aime les romans faux: ce roman est un roman vrai. . . . Il aime les livres qui font semblant d'aller dans le monde: ce livre vient de la rue." Of course, the "truth" that the Goncourt brothers have in mind here is one that complies with what modern semantic logic understands by the "correspondence-theory concept of Truth" (Doležel 1980, 14), and not with D. J. O'Connor's "coherence-theory concept of Truth" (1975), which can be fully applied, however, to non-genetic or formal realism, as we shall presently see.

George J. Becker's useful colllection can provide us with numerous other proofs of the remarkable persistence of genetic realism. It is very revealing, for instance, that the famous "Manifeste des cinque contre *La Terre*," which appeared in *Le Figaro* on August 18, 1887, and which has been interpreted as marking the end of the Médan school—i.e., as a reorientation of naturalism toward a less closed aesthetics, more receptive to symbolism—should attack Zola's most recent work for his departure from true reality, his deficient observation of that reality, and, consequently, his replacement of genetic fidelity with some kind of imposture. This confirms Roman Jakobson's and Fernando Lázaro Carreter's observation that virtually any new literary school asserted its identity by proclaiming that its realistic impulse was more genuine and more accurate than that of its predecessors.

Only a few years before the "Manifeste des cinque," two German naturalists, the brothers Heinrich and Julius Hart, in their essay *Für und gegen Zola*, had maintained that the sole task of literature was to reflect all of reality like a mirror or, according to Becker (1963, 254), "in the meaning of Aristotle's *mimesis*, to mirror and reshape it." Becker's paraphrase again illustrates the connection between realism and mimesis; it also appropriates, for realism, the famous trope of the mirror, of obvious genetic import, coined by Saint-Réal and made popular by the epigraph to Chapter 13 of Stendhal's *Le rouge et le noir* (1831): "Un roman: c'est un miroir qu'on promène le long d'un chemin."

Here I should perhaps note that my term "genetic realism" does not carry any pejorative connotations. It merely describes a textual practice, isolating a theoretical concept to be compared with other such concepts in order to reach a proper understanding of a complex and ineffable phenomenon such as the delicate balance between pure creation and the articulation of reality involved in any literary act. I shall soon have occasion to refine my description of the genetic mode of realist literature, the more vulgar and literalist versions of which cannot be blamed on the genre itself, but on certain obtuse critics and mediocre artists—a feeling equally shared by Harry Levin (1963, 553).

There are, moreover, examples of extraordinary artists, both emulators and critics of Zola's naturalism, who subscribed to a realism that stemmed from their personal confrontation with an observed reality that deserved to be faithfully reproduced, in order to offer their readers a certain truth about nature, the social world, and human beings, entirely opposed to idealistic and romantic humbug. For instance, Leopoldo Alas aspired "to know how to copy the world as it is in its forms and movement; to know how to imitate the likely combination of ordinary accidents; to know how to copy the solidarity in which events, beings, and their works coexist." So the novelist's main talent is "to know how to see and copy" but also, and to no lesser degree, "to know how to construct" (Leopoldo Alas 1982, 142). In turn, Henry James, in one of his most important theoretical texts, "The Art of Fiction" (1884), even as he repeatedly defends the novelist's creative freedom in his controversy with Walter Besant, does not hesitate to affirm: "The only reason for the existence of a novel is that it does attempt to represent life. When it relinquishes this attempt, the same attempt that we see on the canvas of the painter, it will have arrived at a very strange pass" (1884, 46). According to James, "a novel is in its broadest definition a personal, a direct impression of life" (1884, 50); moreover, "you will not write a good novel unless you possess the sense of reality" (1884, 52).

James Miller Jr. (1976) analyzes in detail James's views on reality and the novel, so that I do not need to insist on them here. Nothing would be easier, however, than to trace genetic realism in successive links—from Theodore Dreiser to twentieth-century American naturalism, from European neorealism to the "nouveau roman" and "dirty realism"— preferably rising above such anecdotal attitudes as that of Alain Robbe-Grillet, who made a winter trip to Brittany in order to closely observe the seagulls and the ocean waves so that he could later describe them exactly and "sincerely" in *Le voyeur* (cf. Robbe-Grillet 1963, 181–182).

A genetic concept of realism equally informs Auerbach's *Mimesis*, e.g., when he argues for the indubitable mimetic value of Gregory of Tours's Latin prose in his *History of the Franks*, since the bishop, by virtue of his job, "is professionally in contact with all the people and conditions he writes about. . . . From his activity in the pursuit of his duties, he acquires his ability to observe and the desire to write down what he observes" (Auerbach 1953, 92). Later on, in the chapter on Shakespeare's *Henry IV*, which precedes the one on *Don Quijote*, Auerbach seems to support his view that the Spanish literature of the period was more mimetic than the literature of Elizabethan England with a tautological argument that could be summarized as follows: the Spanish reality was more *realistic* than its English counterpart because of a greater participation of the lower classes in the historical process, due to certain favorable political circumstances (1953, 311–312). For Auerbach, realism is "the serious representation of the social reality of that epoch, based on continuous historical movement" (1953, 486), a critical desideratum that is finally fulfilled in nineteenth-century France with Stendhal and Balzac. For example, he comments on Balzac's Letter of October 1834 to Frau von Hanska (specifically on Balzac's remark about his *Etudes de moeurs*: "Ce ne seront pas des faits imaginaires: ce sera ce qui se passe partout"): "What is expressed here is that the source of his invention is not free imagination but real life, as it presents itself everywhere. Now, in respect to this manifold life, steeped in history, mercilessly represented with all its everyday triviality, practical preoccupations, ugliness, and vulgarity, Balzac has an atttitude such as Stendhal had had before him: in the form determined by its actuality, its triviality, its inner historical laws, he takes it seriously and even tragically. This, since the rise of classical taste, had occurred nowhere—and even before then not in Balzac's practical and historical manner, oriented as it is upon a social self-accounting of man" (1953, 480–481). This citation contains another reason—apart from the absence of a precise theoretical framework—for the objections raised against Auerbach by several theorists, including René Wellek (1954, 303) and Piero Raffa (1967, 319): the exclusive identification of realism with a grave or sublime tone—what John Orr (1977, 4) has called "Auerbach's 'tragic realism.'" But, of course, I have brought it up in the present context mainly because it contains clear references to genetic realism.

Years later, in the context of Marxist literary theory (on which I shall focus in the next section), Stefan Morawski aligns himself in no uncertain terms with genetic realism against its formal counterpart: "Le réalisme comme catégorie, n'exige aucune caractéristique formelle particulière. Il y a pour conditions préalables celles qui concernent seulement la fonction d'une représentation (figurative) de la nature et de la capture de l'essence du phénomène représenté" (Morawski 1963, 71). A program of this kind would provoke numerous objections from formalist criticism, resulting in several fallacies. Of course, it would primarily be guilty of W. K. Wimsatt's famous "intentional fallacy," which is no different from Yvor Winters's "mimetic fallacy" or Bernard de Voto's "literary fallacy" (cf. Harry Levin 1963, 27). As Wimsatt writes: "The Intentional Fallacy is a confusion between the poem and its origins, a special case of what is known to a philosopher as the *Genetic Fallacy* (my emphasis). It begins by trying to derive the standard of criticism from the psychological *cause* of the poem and ends in biography and relativism" (W. K. Wimsatt 1954, 21).

This type of realist text, assuming that its genetic premise were fully accepted, would require an exclusive "hermeneutics of reconstruction" in the manner of Schleiermacher (cf. H. G. Gadamer 1965, 162–173). Here, then, we have introduced a new perspective into our argument, the hermeneutic one, which I consider vital and which has so far been insufficiently brought to bear on the question of realism. From a hermeneutic standpoint, the meaning of the art work can be elucidated only by starting with the world that produced it (cf. Stein Haugom Olsen 1982); i.e., with its origin and genesis—a view advanced by the "positive" hermeneuticians (in contrast to the "negative" ones, in Paul Ricoeur's terminology), such as E. D. Hirsch (1967; 1976) or P. D. Juhl. However, Juhl, who dedicates a whole chapter of a recent book (1980) to the relation of literature to life and truth, denouncing the excesses of the opposite fallacy that completely dissociates literature from both spheres (something that I also deplore), ends up, nevertheless, with an indiscriminate identification between what the text postulates and what the author has seen, thought, or really believed (Juhl 1980, 158–194).

But we have yet to consider the linguistic aspect of genetic realism, directly related to the verbal medium of literary mimesis. To this end we can again turn to Zola, for it is only fit that the most complete theoretical articulation of genetic realism should give language the attention that it deserves. Thus, in "Les romanciers naturalistes" we read: "Je voulais bien une composition simple, une langue nette, quelque chose comme une maison de verre laissant voir les idées à l'intérieur . . . les documents humains donnés dans leur nudité sévère" (*Oeuvres complètes*, XI, Paris: Tchon, 1968, 92). This idea comes from an earlier source, Zola's Letter to Valabrègne (August 18, 1864), in which he develops his theory of the three screens: the classical, the romantic, and the realist. He describes the last of the three as "un simple verre à vitre, très mince, très clair, et qui a la prétention d'être si parfaitement transparent que les images le traversent et se réproduisent ensuite dans leur réalité. L'écran réaliste nie sa propre existence" (cf. Alain de Lattre 1975, 988 ff.). Zola's idea is to hide the form as much as possible, so that its transparency may favor what Hayek calls the "fallacy of conceptual realism," which consists in believing that behind each word there is a designated object corresponding to it, and that the more imperceptible the word becomes, the more presence and corporeality its object will acquire. This "propositional phantom," as Wittgenstein calls it in the *Tractatus*, can be related to a neopositivist type of semantics, influenced by a scientism that believes in the true existence of an objective truth and a solid, unchallengeable world. The main principles of this semantics (some of them cited by Harry Levin—1963, 539—as an epigraph to his last chapter "Realism and reality") are present in the *Tractatus* itself:

2.063.   The total reality is the world.
2.1.   We make to ourselves pictures of facts.
2.12.   The picture is a model of reality.
2.141.   The picture is a fact.
2.1511. Thus the picture is linked with reality; it reaches up to it.
2.15.12. It is like a scale applied to reality.
2.1514. The representing relation consists of the coordinations of the elements of the picture and the things.
2.161.   In the picture and the pictured there must be something identical in order that the one can be a picture of the other at all.
2.17.   What the picture must have in common with reality in order to be able to represent it after its manner—rightly or falsely—is its form of representation.
2.21.   The picture agrees with reality or not; it is right or wrong, true or false.
2.22.   The picture represents what it represents, independently of its truth or falsehood, through the form of representation.
2.221.   What the picture represents is its sense.
2.222.   In the agreement or disagreement of its sense with reality, its truth or falsity consists.
2.223.   In order to discover whether the picture is true or false we must compare it with reality.
3.01.   The totality of true thoughts is a picture of the world.
3.203.   The name means the object. The object is its meaning. ("A" is the same sign as "A.")
4.06.   Propositions can be true or false only by being pictures of the reality. (Wittgenstein 1922, 39–43, 47,71)

These early Wittgensteinean principles represent the embodiment of the referent imitated in the word that designates it, owing to a utopian dissolution of the word itself, a view which parallels that of genetic realism as articulated by Zola and which tips the balance alarmingly toward a notion of content that denies all literariness. In the same vein, there is another linguistic view, recently adopted by some literary scholars as well, which refers to the nature of the verbal sign and which could, in my opinion, be counted as a new argument in favor of a genetic realism that, following Champfleury, proclaims "l'infériorité de la forme et la puissance de l'idée." I am thinking of the opponents of the principle of the arbitrariness of the linguistic sign, who hold that language in general, and literary language in particular, is not exclusively symbolic, but also iconic, to use a Peircean terminology. Among the ablest defenders of this view—Otto Jespersen, J. Damourette and E. Pichon, D. L. Bolinger—one can also include Emile Benveniste (1966, 52), who denies the arbitrariness of the sign from the standpoint of a pragmatics that takes into account the speaker's perspective, for whom there is "entre la langue et la réalité adéquation complète: le signe recouvre et commande la réalité; mieux, il *est* cette réalité."

From the same pragmatic standpoint, one must acknowledge that the protocol of a non-conventional type of communication such as the literary one is considerably different from that of a conventional type, and it was first Roman Jakobson (1971), and then literary theorists such as William Wimsatt (1975), who raised this question within a specifically aesthetic framework. Jakobson, for instance, mentions the case of the theater, employing arguments reminiscent of Thomas Twining's (stage words are icons of the words uttered in the course of the human action to be imitated), and pointing out other clear cases of syntactic, phonetic, diagramatic, and visual iconicity, to be found in literary texts, particularly in poetry. (For the relation between iconicity and realism, see Gianfranco Bettetini's study, 1971.)

Regardless of the validity of Peirce's assertion that symbols, icons, and indices are not autonomous signs, closed in themselves, without hybrid combinations among them, I believe that the basic structure of the linguistic expression rests upon Saussurean conventionality and that extending the particular and concrete literary procedures in which iconicity plays a role to the entire literary phenomenon would be a methodological setback rather than advance in clarifying the issue of genetic realism, which would then be understood in as unsophisticated a manner as possible.

The Theory of Reflection

Among the archetypal expressions of genetic realism it has become a commonplace to cite the theory of reflection formulated by the advocates of socialist realism, but we shall see that this theory is richer and more complex than is generally recognized.

On the other hand, it is true that socialist realism itself is largely based on the genetic principle; witness, for instance, the concept of "the typical," found in Marx and Engels's letters (1954) to Ferdinand Lasalle about his historical drama, *Franz von Sickingen*. Moreover, Engels's 1887 Letter to the social novelist Margaret Harkness (upon the publication of her novel, *Mister Grant*), in addition to a clear and concise definition of "the typical," contains an argument in favor of genetic realism that subsequent critics will cite again and again. Thus, Engels writes: "The only thing that I find questionable about your story is that it is not realistic enough. Realism, in my opinion, means, in addition to an accuracy of details, the exact representation of typical characters in typical circumstances" (Marx and Engels 1954, 165). Then, referring to *La comédie humaine* by Balzac, whom he considers "a master of realism infinitely greater than all the Zolas *passés, presents, et à venir*," Engels argues that the mimetic value of French society depicted in the novel derives from the expressive vigor latent in the reality observed by the author, who, precisely because of what he sees around him, is "compelled to go against his own class sympathies and political prejudices." For Engels, this fact represents "one of the great triumphs of realism" (1954, 167); of genetic realism, one should add, for which everything is based

on the power of reality itself, on the artist's capacity of observation, and finally, on his sincerity, which will prevent him
from misrepresenting what appears before him and might dis-
please or not interest him.

A rudimentary but colorful articulation of the same program can be found in Stalin's formula, enthusiastically glossed
by Zhdanov in 1934, according to which the writer must be an
engineer of human souls, which basically implies that he must
rely on reality and know it thoroughly so that he can depict it
accurately in his work (cf. G. J. Becker 1963, 487ff; Stefan
Morawsky 1974, 287–288; and Carlos Reis 1987, 159–195).

Realism, then, is undoubtedly the cornerstone of Marxist
aesthetics, for which, according to Christopher Caudwell
(1937: 188), "art is the product of society, as a pearl is the
product of the oyster." The most typical formulation of its
postulates can be found in the aforementioned theory of reflection, especially as developed by Georg Lukács. Lukács starts
from the materialist postulate of the alterity of real things,
the plenitude of the objective world vis-à-vis the subjectivity
of the I; in other words, from the existence of a reality independent of our minds. As we read in "Art and Objective
Truth" (1934), "Any conception of the outside world is nothing but a reflection of human consciousness in a world that
exists independently of that conception. Of course, this fundamental fact of the relation between consciousness and being
equally applies to the authentic reflection of reality" (Lukács
1955, 11). Such authentic reflection allows us to conceive of
aesthetic creation, in Ernst Fischer's words, "not as the arbitrary freewill of man, but as a homologon of reality" (Lukács,
Adorno, Jakobson, Fischer, and Barthes 1969, 105).

Later on, in his *Aesthetics* (1963, 472 ff.), Lukács devotes
to the issue of reflection a whole section (VI. General Features
of the Relation beween Subject and Object in Aesthetics), in
Chapter 10, "Problems of Mimesis." He also links his theory
of reflection to an open concept of *mimesis* that is closer to
the Platonic than to the Aristotelian postulates, and he
defends the full artistic relevance of objective idealism for
contemporary creation: "Antiquity, for which the doctrine of
reflection did not yet imply the materialist stigma, but—as

in Plato—constituted a basic element of objective idealism, has unreservedly acknowledged, through its great thinkers (including Plato and Aristotle), imitation as a foundation of life, thought, and artistic activity. Only when the philosophical idealism of the modern era saw itself constrained by materialism to assume a defensive position and reject the doctrine of reflection in order to save, vis-à-vis Being, the dogma of the priority of conscious being—in the sense of the production of the former by the latter—only then did the doctrine of reflection become an academic taboo" (1963, 8).

In any case, according to Lukács, "the mission of art consists in the restoration of the concrete . . . through the direct sensible evidence" (1955, 32) of a reality conceived "as something not invented, but simply discovered" (1955, 187). Here, reproductive fidelity and the apprehension of details are vitally important, for details are "authentic reflections of reality" (Lukács 1958, 64). But such details, precisely insofar as they are typical, will allow, if chosen wisely, a transcendental leap toward the essential, a leap that Lukács, as well as other Marxist theorists, demands. The work of art will necessarily offer a slice or fragment of reality, but ultimately it must not separate this slice from the totality of social life. As Lukács writes in "The Question of Realism" (1938), "if literature is indeed a particular form of reflection of objective reality, it is concerned with apprehending that reality as it actually is, without limiting itself to reproducing what directly seems to be. If the writer aims at capturing and representing reality as it is, i.e., if the author is genuinely realistic, then the problem of the objective totality of reality plays a crucial role" (1955, 293).

There remains an apparent contradiction between the decidedly genetic and mimetic impulse of Marxist reflection and the obvious effort on the part of its theoreticians to prevent it from being understood simplistically as a mere mechanical transposition of reality—apprehended in its typical details—into literature. Lenin himself, in his *Philosophical Notebooks*—cited by Lukács in the first volume of his *Aesthetics* (1963, 66)—has warned that the human understanding's approach of a specific object in order to abstract from it a copy or concept is never a simple procedure, "immediate, specular, and dead, but rather a complex, discontinuous, and zigzagging action"—a judgment that Engels also shares in his *Dialektik der Natur* (Lukács 1963, 85). So Lukács's notion of reflection implies a genetic realism that is both truthful and selective, both intensifying and totalizing. This is the best proof that he does not simplistically equate literature with reality-world-life, as certain theoretical and artistic versions of naturalism do. In this regard, Lukácsian aesthetics has been treated rather unfairly even by some Marxists, such as T. W. Adorno (Lukács, Adorno, Jakobson, Fischer, and Barthes 1969, 88). A balanced reassessment of Lukács's genetic realism will perhaps allow us to defend some of its earlier versions as well.

In "The Question of Realism," Lukács's theoretical statements are illuminating to us beyond the limited scope of Marxist realism and its theory of reflection. They become even more enlightening in a later work, *Wider den missverstandenen Realismus* (1958): "Marxism places the reflection of objective reality in the center of its aesthetics more decisively and completely than any previous aesthetics. But this position is closely related to the fundamental elements of the Marxist vision of the world. In the eyes of a marxist, the path to socialism is the very course of social reality; any typical phenomenon, whether objective or subjective, is an important element . . . the correct evaluation of these phenomena is a vital issue for any socialist thinker" (Lukács 1958, 125). This is the reason why, according to Lukács, socialist realism is superior to all other realisms (or all other genetic realisms, one should rather say): "The ideological basis of that superiority lies in the clear vision that the writer gets from the socialist conception of the world, from the socialist perspective, enabling him to embrace, reflect, and describe social being and consciousness, man and human relations, the problems of life and their solutions, in a more profound way than any previous conceptions of the world had made it possible" (Lukács 1958, 146).

What Lukacs means here is that reality and the literary text reflecting it are not related in a direct or dyadic manner, according to the medieval principle of "aliquid stat pro aliquo"; rather, there is a third discourse that intervenes between them, in the manner of Peirce's "interpretant," which places itself between the referential object or *designatum* and the sign or *representamen*. This third discourse, in Lukács's theory, is an ideology, an essentialist interpretation of reality called Marxism (cf. Althusser, in *Pour Marx* [Paris: Maspero, 1965])—a Marxism, moreover, that is, in Terry Lovell's words, "both an ontology and an epistemology" (Lovell 1980, 22). Therefore, the accusations of mechanicity and naivity of *Weltanschauung* levelled against Lukács's genetic realism, when they are justified at all, concern less his general idea of reflection—which is fundamentally triadic rather than binary—than the reductive content of his third discourse (Marxism) that sifts the details of reality through an ideologically monistic lens. As far as the basic structure of the mimetic relation is concerned, Lukács situates himself within the purest Aristotelian tradition.

In fact, Aristotelian mimesis itself has only recently been linked to Peircean semiotics and the concept of interpretant (cf. Mieke Bal 1982). According to this semiotic view, for Aristotle, the mimetic text does not replace or represent the objective action that it imitates except through the indirect mediation of common opinion, i.e., of what the audience considers real, regardless whether it is or not. The often-quoted and glossed passages of the *Poetics*—from Karl R. Popper (1964; 1968) to Gérard Genot (1968) and Roland Barthes (1968)—that argue the artistic desirability of the probable impossibility over the improbable possibility (60a 26–27; 61b 11–13) do endorse the Lukácsian approach as well, because, as Gérard Genette shrewdly points out, "cette 'opinion', réelle ou supposée, c'est assez précisément ce que l'on nommerait aujourd'hui une idéologie, c'est-à-dire un corpus de maximes et de préjugés qui constitue tout à la fois une vision du monde et un système de valeurs" (1968, 6).

If one were to accept Genette's argument, then even the most genetically faithful realism involves a decisive element of world outlook (and here I use genetic realism in my sense of the term, which excludes its radically literal interpretation as a mere photographic reproduction, for literalist programs rarely produce satisfying aesthetic results). Aristotle regards as realistic the literary creation that complies with certain social conventions, not so much with respect to the artistic form of expression as to the artistic content and the external referent to which these conventions point. Here, as elsewhere, Aristotle largely follows his master Plato who, in *Laws* (660a), decrees that the poet should not compose anything contrary to what his fellow citizens regard as legal and just, or fair and good. This Platonic decree can also be related to what Northrop Frye calls the "myth of concern": "The myth of concern exists to hold society together so far as words can help to do this. For it, truth and reality are not directly connected with reasoning or evidence, but are socially established. What is true, for concern, is what society does and believes in response to authority; and a belief, so far as a belief is verbalized, is a statement of willingness to participate in a myth of concern" (1971, 36).

Thus, paradoxically, socialist realism is the faithful reflection—through artistic means—of a world ideologically interpreted in the light of Marxism. According to Lukács, the most realistic literary work is the one which, starting from a concrete reality that engenders the genetic principle of the work intending to represent it, will project its reflection (i.e., the reflection of reality toward the text, and the reflection of the text in relation to reality) through a third discourse, or "interpretant," called Marxist ideology. So, what can be more logical than Thomas E. Lewis's parallel (1979) between the concept of "referent" in the Marxist theory of reflection—which Althusser perhaps articulates even more clearly than Lukács—and Umberto Eco's semiotics, essentially faithful to Peirce's principles? The two systems do not presuppose a relation between sign and referent, but one between sign and a convention understood as a "cultural unit" or an ideology—"a system of representation of images, concretized in specific practices" (Lewis 1979, 470)—that is projected upon the referent. Hence, Althusserian Marxist epistemology—the aesthetic consequences of which cannot be explored in the present context—"subscribes to the same complex of assertions about the relations of thought to the real that figures in the semiotic notion (at least as defined by Eco) of the relation of language to the real expressed in the concepts of the interpretant and meaning as a cultural unit" (Lewis 1979, 469).

In addition to the studies devoted to the Aristotelian idea of verisimilitude, scholarship on the mimetic tradition from Aristotle to modern realism (cf. Jan Bruck 1982, 191–195) reveals how one of the eighteenth-century exegetes of the *Poetics*, J. C. Gottsched, in *Versuch einer kritischen Dichtkunst vor die Deutschen* (1730), refers the genetic origin of *mimesis* not so much to an objective, physical, or material reality as to the rational structure of the world, informed by the spirit of eighteenth-century Enlightenment, that is, by another "ideology." Two other interesting, hitherto unpublished studies (at least as far as I know) follow the same line of research: The first one, *Fiction and Reference*, also by Thomas E. Lewis (1985), develops a thesis similar to that of his other book (1979), but this time in relation to Terry Eagleton's Neomarxist critical views. The second one, Beate Wolff's doctoral dissertation (University of Bielefeld, 1971) on "Mimesis. Genese und Wirkung des Theorems von der Kunst als Nachahmung der Natur"—cited and discussed by Siegfried J. Schmidt (1980c, 82)—interprets Aristotle's notion of *mimesis* less as a direct reproduction of reality than as a factor of ideological induction at the time when audiences perceive and understand this reality. Michael Riffaterre (1984, 159) aptly expresses a related idea ("The mimetic text is not composed of words referring to things but words referring to systems of signs that are ready-made textual units"), which is equally present in Julia Kristeva's earlier theory of verisimilitude as a discourse resembling the discourse resembling reality, i.e., as a problem of meaning, rather than one of objectivity or correspondence (1968, 61–62).

The Construction of Reality

Nowadays it is widely accepted, apart from any interpretant derived from a coherent and closed ideology (be it the eighteenth-century rationalist vision of reality or dialectic materialism), that the real is not something ontologically solid and univocal but, rather, a construction of both individual and collective consciousness. Nelson Goodman is the staunchest champion of a "constructivist" philosophy that precludes the existence of a real world prior to the activity of the human mind or—as another "constructivist," Jerome Bruner, argues in his influential *Actual Minds, Possible Worlds* (1986)—prior to the symbolic language that the human mind employs in order to create worlds.

From this perspective, one must necessarily accept not only the conventionality of the linguistic sign, but also that of reality itself. In fact, modern sociology of knowledge equally understands human reality as something socially constituted and makes it its scientific task to explore the process by which such a phenomenon occurs, a process in which language plays an important role (cf. Peter Berger and Thomas Luckmann 1973). Applying the principles of this sociology to our discipline, Virgil Nemoianu (1984, 293) speaks of "societal models" interposed between reality and mimetic literature, defining them as "cross sections of reality, their impetus coming from a coherent system of values."

As Susana Reisz de Rivarola points out in an important study on literary fiction (1979, 144), "the inclusion of a certain phenomenon within the realm of reality or irreality" varies "from community to community and from epoch to epoch," and this fact affects the consideration of literature, because what can be called "the collective experience of reality" mediatizes the reader's response to the world evoked by the literary work. By way of an imaginative example, she offers a comparison between Ovid's and Kafka's *Metamorphoses*, both of which present situations equally alien to the daily reality of a European in the first century A.D. or in the twentieth century. But, in its time, Ovid's work was not considered a form of fantastic fiction, despite the fact that it presents a nymph turning into a laurel tree when chased by a god, whereas Kafka's is considered as such in our time, just because it presents an obscure salesman turning into a monstrous insect. A similar example, I believe, could be a hypothetical book of fabulous travels, in the manner of Anthony Diogenes's

Wonders from Beyond Thule, but composed before Pythagoras of Samos (or even after him, because his pioneering hypothesis of the Earth's sphericity did not *ipso facto* topple the opposite belief); this narrative would include a journey to the West from which one would return to the Greek isles from the East, so that it would appear totally implausible to its ancient audience by virtue of the cosmological theory of the circularity (rather than sphericity) of the Earth.

Constructivist epistemology, whose materialist and relativist orientation is very obvious, advances along the same lines, as one can see from Paul Watzlawick's very interesting collection (1984), entitled *The Invented Reality: How Do We Know What We Believe We Know? Contributions to Constructivism.* Siegfried J. Schmidt (1980b; 1984), relying on Humberto R. Maturana (1970; 1980) and others, has applied this kind of epistemological constructivism to the literary act. His basic assumption is that each perceiving subject "produces the world he lives in by living in it" (S. J. Schmidt 1984, 258), so that reality, both in real life and in fiction, is always a "construct" shaped as "models"—or "models of institutional representation," as Jenaro Taléns writes in the foreword to J. M. Company-Ramón's *La realidad como sospecho* (1986, 9). None of these constructions has ontological reality, but those that become more adjusted than others start being "treated as standard elements of the OWN" (Schmidt 1984, 267) or the "ortho-world-model," i.e., as socialized models of reality and the world (Schmidt 1980b, 530–531). This discovery that reality is not very real represents, as has been noted by J. F. Lyotard and others, one more symptom of the postmodern condition.

The latest semiotic theories (cf. Jenaro Taléns 1986, 12–13) also acknowledge three steps or levels of textual space present during the complex operation that is the production of meaning: the textual space *par excellence* would obviously be that of the novel, painting, poem, or motion picture; on a second level, there are the textual representations open to several possibilities of organization and fixation, such as drama or a musical score; but the last space (or the first, depending on your perspective) would belong to reality itself, which already signifies, but which lacks organization and fixation, being at the discretion of those imposed by the other two textual spaces.

Bertold Brecht, another illustrious literary practitioner and theorist influenced by Marxism, is an equally good example of the problematic of genetic realism in all its aspects, with an added element concerning his notion of form, which is at the core of his famous controversy with Georg Lukács and is, therefore, of great interest in the present context. Brechtian realism, like the Lukácsian one, has a genetic starting point. The first of Brecht's "Theses for Proletarian Literature" reads: "Fight by writing! Show that you fight! Energetic realism! Reality is on your side, be on its side! Let life speak! Don't do it violence!" (Brecht 1967, 276). Later, in "On the Label 'Socialist Realism,'" Brecht concludes: "Write the truth! Be realistic!" (Brecht 1967, 283). And when he assesses Maxim Gorky's literary value, he praises him especially because "everything he narrates is true: he has seen it, and of course has seen it well, and his account has falsified nothing" (Brecht 1967, 335).

Here Brecht seems at first to return to a naturalistic approach: there is a solid and objective reality, confronted by a writer endowed with a mimetic will and fine qualities as an exhaustive observer. But he, just like Lukacs, interposes ideology between reality and the text. For example, he makes a highly enlightening comment with regard to the theory of realistic detail and its totalizing import: "The true meaning of the word 'typical,' considered important by the Marxists, is: historically meaningful" (Brecht 1967, 409). In other words, we have again the interpretant of raw reality. Obviously, for Brecht, "*Realist* means: that which discovers the social causal complex/ unmasks the dominant points of view as the points of view of those who dominate/ writes from the point of view of the class that has the most extensive solutions for the most pressing problems within human society/ stresses the moment of development/ makes possible the concrete and the abstract" (Brecht 1967, 237–238).

But Brecht's originality within the Marxist theory of genetic realism consists precisely in what makes him disagree with Lukács: the question of form. The German playwright blames the Hungarian philosopher for his basic lack of interest in the purely artistic aspects of realistic creation, excepting the occasions on which Lukács wants to impose the most conventional and traditional literary forms upon it, at the expense of innovative and experimental ones. In this sense, Lukács—in the manner of Zola, which I have also related to that of early Wittgenstein—wants genetic realism to possess a hardly perceptible, if not altogether transparent, linguistic tool. In the wake of the debate around the expressionism of 1938, Brecht vehemently opposes Lukács's normative and aesthetically conservative rigidity (Brecht 1967, 213). And precisely because he is an artist, he has to defend the world of artistic form in terms that, without breaking with genetic realism, definitely point to an alternative mode of understanding literary mimesis: "In art, the form plays a great role. It is not everything, but it is so much that ignoring it destroys a work. It is not something external, something that the artist imposes on the content; it is so much part of the content that the artist can often present it as the content itself, for in creating an art work, the formal elements most frequently come into being together with, or at times even before, the theme" (Brecht 1967, 403).

Brecht's cogent objections to Lukács have variously been adopted by Western semioticians sympathetic to Marxism, such as Piero Raffa (1967, 283), as well as by East European researchers and academics, such as those whose critical studies were gathered in a nineteen-sixties anthology by the Hungarian scholars Béla Köpeczi and Péter Juhász (1966). Likewise, Dimitri S. Likhachov, a scholar from the former Soviet Union, argued in 1971 that realism was a matter of method rather than style, being Protean in form, and therefore should not be identified with any specific, rigorously defined, style—a view that is not far from the one I have proposed at the beginning of this chapter.

2

FORMAL REALISM AND BEYOND

We shall now turn to "conscious realism" (Grant 1970) or "formal realism" (Sörbom 1966), which Ian Watt (1957, 31–32) had already largely defined when arguing that the realism of the nineteenth-century English narrative implied less an indiscriminate *mimesis* of the world in which the novelists lived than a complex of literary techniques with which these novelists artistically constructed their fictional worlds.

In fact, despite a continuous mimetic literary tradition originating in Plato and Aristotle, there have always been views, such as Hegel's, that consider the attempt artificially to remake, through aesthetic means, what already exists in the external world as a useless and superfluous exercise, doomed to failure. One should point out that even in the century of genetic realism par excellence, and among some of the writers who were closely identified with it, there were highly authoritative voices defending the autonomy of the literary work and granting a purely creative status to the reality presented in it.

I shall, then, speak of formal or immanent realism, in contradistinction to genetic realism, but I shall certainly not ascribe to it (as I have done in the case of the latter) a "hermeneutic of reconstruction"—the most logical way of projecting, by correspondence, the internal world described in the text upon the real, objective world in which this text originated. Instead, I shall introduce Hans Georg Gadamer's hermeneutic principle of "aesthetic differentiation" (1965, 76–78), which, according to Gadamer, implicitly makes abstraction of "everything in which a work is rooted (its original context of life, and the religious or secular function which gave it its significance)," or the work's "extra-aesthetic elements, such as purpose, function, the meaning of its content." In this sense, "through 'aesthetic differentiation,' the art work loses its place and the world to which it belongs insofar as it belongs to aesthetic consciousness." E. D. Hirsch (1967), one of the most ardent opponents of this Gadamerian principle, calls it "metaphorical," because it grants the text its own life, relatively free of the author and his intention.

Flaubert and Formal Realism

Perhaps Gustave Flaubert is the first author who became fully aware of the formal or immanent realism that he was in effect practising. His ideas in this regard are recorded in his correspondence (Gustave Flaubert 1973; 1980), e.g., in the famous letter of January 16, 1852 to Louise Collet, to whom he confesses his desire to write "un livre sur rien, un livre sans attache extérieur qui se tiendrait de lui-même par la force interne de son style, comme la terre sans être soutenue se tient en l'air" (G. Flaubert 1980, 31); or in his letter to Turgenev, twenty-five years later, with the round statement that for him reality is nothing but a "diving board."

"I do not transcribe, I construct," Alain Robbe-Grillet (1963, 182) reports Flaubert to have repeatedly said, a provocative claim echoed in a letter of March 18, 1857 to Mademoiselle Leroyer de Chantepie (Flaubert 1980, 691–692), according to which *Madame Bovary* had nothing to do with life or the author's experiences or feelings. That did not prevent Flaubert from writing to Louise Collet (Letter of July 22, 1853. Flaubert 1980, 387–388) that reality fitted his fiction *a posteriori* when he came across a real speech in the *Journal de Rouen* that sounded just like the one he had earlier composed for his prefect in the scene of "les comices agricoles" in *Madame Bovary*. A good argument to justify, if this were possible, Oscar Wilde's brilliant hyperbole: "External Nature imitates Art." (For a collection of references to realism in Flaubert's letters, see Becker 1963, 89–96.)

Among the naturalists there are also indications that the evolution of genetic realism was leading them toward this formal-immanent type, which rehabilitates the imagination vis-à-vis observation and which postulates, for the literary work, not a pre-existent external reality, but a created one, simultaneous with the work and constituted in unison with it. In his preface to *Les frères Zemganno* (1879), Edmond de Goncourt confesses to having composed his work in a state of mind in which "la vérité trop vrai m'était antipatique à moi aussi." But the most interesting testimony in this regard is probably that of Guy de Maupassant in his foreword to *Pierre et Jean*, published nine years after Goncourt's book. Maupassant begins by acknowledging that the only thing accessible to us is to create an illusion of the world (Yeats says, in the same spirit, that "Man can embody truth but he cannot know it"); that the realist author's mission is simply to reproduce this illusion as faithfully as possible with all the means at his disposal; and that the greatest artists are those who impose their particular illusion upon humanity at large.

So Maupassant inverts the terms of genetic realism with the implicit assertion that, as Richard Brinkmann (1957, 298) puts it, the only objective expression is subjective experience ("Das Subjektive, das subjektive Erleben, die subjektive Erkenntniss, der subjektive Trieb sind—zugespitzt formuliert—das einzig Objektive"). Maupassant implicitly moves from an ontologically positive epistemology that supports the literary work to a relativist, existentialist, phenomenological, or constructivist one, in which the cognitive I is the sole source and evidence of reality for the mimetic products of his imagination. He concludes his argument with a statement that would deserve a separate commentary: "Faire vrai consiste donc à donner l'illusion complète du vrai. . . . J'en conclus que les Réalistes de talent devraient s'appeller plutôt des Illusionistes."

So far, we have pointed out two fundamental aspects of formal or immanent realism: the role of the artist in the production of an autonomous reality and the illusory character of this reality. Let us examine these aspects on by one.

The Author As Creator

For genetic realism the writer has a no less crucial function, emphasized by such formulas as that of Stalin ("engineer of human souls") or that of Zola, which precedes and inspires the former. According to Zola, the novelist is in all respects comparable to the scientist: "Je citerai encore cette image de Claude Bernard, qui m'a beaucoup frappé: 'L'expérimentateur est le juge d'instruction de la nature.' Nous autres romanciers, nous sommes les juges d'instruction des hommes et de leurs passions" (Zola 1971, 65). But, in the case of genetic realism, the writer's importance derives from his position as an observer of and experimenter with a total and solvent reality that only he can significantly imitate and convey for his readers' apprehension. In sum, genetic realism implies a realism that originates both in reality and in the writer's objective capturing of that reality.

By contrast, in formal or immanent realism, since there is no external reference, everything is centered on the author and his relation with the text. Flaubert himself supports this statement, for example, in his much-cited *boutade*, "*Madame Bovary* c'est moi*,*" or in the analogy he draws, in his letter to Mademoiselle Leroyer de Chantepie, between the artist and God, both being invisible although omnipotent within their creations ("L'artiste doit être dans son oeuvre comme Dieu dans la création, invisible et tout-puissant; qu'on le sente partout, mais qu'on ne le voie pas," G. Flaubert 1980, 691). For, indeed, since immanent artistic reality is not a copy of external reality, it can be justified only as the author's product through the literary forms.

Flaubert's ambitious analogy seems to have originated in Florence at the end of the fifteenth century, specifically in Cristoforo Landino's 1481 commentary on Dante (see Abrams 1953, 482–505). Tasso also says: "Non merita nome di creatore se non Iddio ed il Poeta" (Abrams 1953, 483); and the Italian and English Neo-Platonists, including Sir Phillip Sydney, maintain that the artist, like God, is the creator of a second Nature—an idea that Goethe includes, in turn, in his dialogue, *Über die Wahrheit und Wahrscheinlichkeit der Kunstwerke* (1797). Here I cannot trace the whole history of the notion of the artist as demiurge, which extends at least as far as André Malraux's *Les voix du silence* ("les grand artistes ne sont pas les transcripteurs du monde, ils en sont les rivaux"). It is nevertheless one of the key elements for a thorough theoretical understanding of immanent or formal realism.

Jacques Derrida contributes to this theoretical understanding when, in a collective volume focusing on the question of *mimesis* from a deconstructive perspective, he writes: "L'artiste n'imite pas les choses dans la nature, ou si l'on veut dans la *natura naturata,* mais les actes de la *natura naturans,* les opérations de la *physis.* Mais puisq'une analogie a déja fait de la *natura naturans* l'art d'un sujet auteur et, on peut même le dire, d'un dieu artiste, la *mimesis* déploie l'identification de l'acte humain à l'acte divin. D'une liberté à une autre" (Jacques Derrida and others 1975, 67). Thus, according to Derrida, the true *mimesis* does not involve two produced realities (with the reality inside the work becoming a reflection of the external one), but two producing subjects and two operations of production. The writer imitates nothing but God's creative freedom, and the analogy between the two creators "n'est pas seulement un rapport de proportionnalité ou un rapport entre deux—deux sujets, deux origines, deux productions. Le procès analogique est aussi une remontée vers le *logos.* L'origine est le *logos.* L'origine de l'analogie, ce dont procède et vers quoi fait retour l'analogie c'est le *logos,* raison et parole, source comme bouche et embouchure" (1975, 74).

The other fundamental aspect that distinguishes immanent or formal realism from the purely genetic kind is the notion of illusion, present in Maupassant's prologue and also, as a central theme, in Ernst H. Gombrich's very influential *Art and Illusion* (1957). Gombrich's thesis coincides with Maupassant's argument in the preface to *Pierre et Jean* insofar as it claims that all art, even the kind unanimously regarded as realistic, is based on mimetic illusion, rather than on mimetic correspondence or reproduction. The illusion ultimately relies on the use of certain formal conventions and its compliance with the laws of learning in visual perception, depending on the historical moment and the specific culture of a given society, as Gombrich shows in the case of Constable's 1876 painting, "Wivenhoe Park, Essex."

In the same line of research, Nelson Goodman (1968) vigorously champions a conventionalist and formalist concept of realism that is completely anti-geneticist. According to Goodman, the realism of an artistic representation does not reside in any "type of likeness to reality," because, as Gombrich has demonstrated, there is no such thing as an innocent eye. Rather, "an efficient representation and description require invention. They are creative. . . . To say that nature imitates art means very little. Nature is a product of art and language" (Goodman 1968, 49). Consequently, realism is a relative phenomenon, "determined by the normal system of representation of a given culture or person at a given time" (Goodman 1968, 52). Menachem Brinker goes even further by claiming, in his discussion of Gombrich and Goodman (1983b, 275), that a thing can not only represent any other thing, but also be a realist imitation of it. As Brinker argues in a companion article published in the same year (1983, 254–255), this is so because the realist impression or effect depends upon the artistic conventions employed, or form, the audience's habits and expectations, or reception, as well as its beliefs about the section of reality represented, or world outlook/ ideology (cf. also Thomas G. Pavel 1985).

A similar conception underlies Paul Ricoeur's reassessment of Aristotelian *mimesis* (1981), which dislocates this notion from the aesthetic realm of the duplicated presence of things, projecting it onto the pragmatic field of production, or *poiesis*. According to Ricoeur, this is a complex process, involving three phases: "prefiguration," or the socialized model of the imitated world; "configuration," or the emergence of the text itself; and "transfiguration or refiguration," or the act of reading the text. These three phases are three forms of praxis—for Ricoeur's theory, let me emphasize again, is thoroughly pragmatic—so that I shall have occasion to return to them later on in this study.

Gombrich's and Goodman's theory of aesthetic illusion mentioned here has a direct application to literature, despite its origin in the theory of painting. It precludes the idea that the verbal symbol as literary medium may possess the utopian value of an icon—a hypothesis that I have previously considered in relation to genetic realism. If valiant conventionalists such as Gombrich and Goodman go so far as to deny the iconic power of the plastic arts, how could one do less for the verbal work of art? María del Carmen Bobes Naves (1985, 328–330), in elaborating a general theory of the novel based on *La Regenta*—one of the archetypal showcases of European realism—has convincingly demolished the utopian belief that words have the ability to copy extralinguistic objects rather than other words. According to her, "the concept of mimesis as a 'photographic copy,' so common among realist and naturalist critics, as well as the socialist 'theory of reflection,' is based on premises that do not belong to literary science. . . . The novel is not a transposition of reality" (Bobes Naves 1985, 16).

Likewise, Michael Riffaterre concludes his study of descriptive literature (the literary genre that arguably possesses the most "pictorial will," as it were) by saying: "le genre descriptif, plus que toute autre forme littéraire, semblait devoir s'ouvrir sur la réalité. Il n'est rien: toutes les formes de la mimésis n'y font autre chose que créer une *illusion* de *réalité*" (Riffaterre 1972, 30). Shortly before Riffaterre, Roland Barthes brilliantly makes the same point in *S/Z*. According to him, "Toute description littéraire est une vue," because it requires that the realist writer place his originally empty frame upon a collection of objects that would otherwise be inaccessible to his painting by means of words: "pour pouvoir en parler, il faut que l'écrivain, par un rite initial, transforme d'abord le 'réel' en objet peint (encadré)," that is, into an already conventionalized representation. So "le réalisme (bien mal nommé, en tout cas souvent mal interprété) consiste non à copier le réel, mais à copier une copie (peinte) du réel." That is why realism ""ne peut être dit 'copieur' mais plutôt 'pasticheur' (par une *mimesis* seconde, il copie ce qu'est déja copie)" (Barthes 1970, 61). In other words, what realist fiction presents as a real body or object is already a copy of a model articulated by artistic codes and conventions.

Riffaterre's most recent book, oxymoronically entitled *Fictional Truth* (1990), reiterates Barthes's arguments when it states that "narrative truth" is a purely linguistic phenomenon, resulting from the skillful use of certain techniques or "truth devices (Riffaterre 1990, 53) through which the text does not impose the evidence of truth, but rather establishes a verbal representation of reality. The immanent or formal realism understood in this fashion proceeds from a construction, rather than from a transparent transposition of a pre-existing alterity. If, as Todorov (1975, 417) points out, the novelists create rather than imitate reality, the most innovative modern artists are busy replacing the "mimetic principle" with the "constructive principle" even in the theatre, the genre with the highest degree of iconicity (cf. Raffa 1967, 117–118).

The Excesses of Immanentism

The concept of formal realism in literature avoids the perils of genetic mechanicism, interpreting the work in terms of specifically artistic parameters more proper to its essential nature than any external ones, but it carries inside it a germ of total dissociation between the created world and reality itself. Aggravated by the most radical immanentism, it leads us into an opposite dead-end alley. For example, a poor understanding and application of formalist theory produced these negative effects in the study of literature during the nineteen sixties, against which there was a significant backlash in the following decade. The repeated formalist assertions about an absolute lack of referent in literature provoked explicit statements affirming the opposite, but now such statements made a distinction between the real and fictitious character of the referent and showed respect for textual immanency. A good example of this balanced approach was Georges Lavis's "Le texte littéraire, le réferent, le réel, le vrai" (1971), which refuted a formalist study by Michel Arrivé, without returning in the slightest to "le décalque pur et simple de la réalité" (Lavis 1971, 22). In turn, Tzvetan Todorov, an introducer and translator of the Russian formalists in Western Europe, affirmed that "to investigate the 'truth' of a literary text is a non-pertinent operation, and means reading it as a non-literary text" (Ducrot and Todorov 1972, 301); at the same time, however, he acknowledged the unquestionably representational nature of verbal art, in his study on fantastic literature (1970, 64).

John Orr charged that the excesses of the dissociation between literature and reality, which he attributed to the French structuralists of *Tel Quel* and the heirs of the Russian formalist school, had brought us to the brink of a dangerous reductionism and, what is worse, had led literature to a denial of humanism (1977, 30). René Girard also appeared to agree with these charges: "Literature for the sake of literature starts to look like sex for the sake of sex, and any other thing for its own sake, in other words, like some kind of idolatry. The dead-end alley is always the same" (1978, 226). Finally, Juan Oleza (1976, 24–66) takes a similar position in Spain.

This kind of reasonable attitude, far from fading away, has increasingly reasserted itself in recent years, producing new and significant critiques of extreme immanentism, without returning to the geneticist interpretations that current theoretical-critical thought has left far behind. It is no longer unusual to encounter books such as Raymond Tallis's *In Defence of Realism* (1988, 219), which concludes that realism is one of the "regulative ideas" (in the Kantian sense) of literature, and the supreme one in the case of fiction. Here one can also mention the controversy between Murray Krieger (1984) and E. H. Gombrich (1984) in *Critical Inquiry*, centering around Gombrich's book *The Image and the Eye* (1982). Krieger reproaches Gombrich for moving away from the relativist and conventionalist interpretation of pictorial signs in *Art and Illusion* and favoring a closer relationship of these signs with the reality that they denote (M. Krieger 1984, 191). For his part, Gombrich, who does seem to have shifted from absolute immanentism and aesthetic economy toward an artistic mimesis that depends on reality, replies spiritedly that the school of literary criticism to which Krieger belongs seems to praise his *Art and Illusion* without having read it, for it is a misunderstanding of its intention to take it as a manifesto of "an aesthetics in which the notions of reality and of nature had no place" (Gombrich 1984, 195).

Another very influential journal of literary theory, *Poetics Today*, has published an entire issue and several additional articles to show the same change of direction that is represented by Gombrich. In a monograph issue about fiction and reference, Peter Brooks (1983, 73) argues that the various formalisms of the nineteen sixties and seventies have produced "a certain weariness," recently countered by "a certain yearning for the return of the referent." And two years later, Shimon Sandbank raises the same question in the realm of poetry. Confronted with the "self-referentiality of literature," Sandbank (1985, 464) asks himself: "Should the referential function, too, enjoy a critical revival?" This revival has undoubtedly taken place, because opinions such as that of Leo H. Hoek (1981, 146) are no longer unacceptable: "On peut affirmer que le texte littéraire n'est pas immédiatement référentiel mais entretient pourtant des relations avec le monde extérieur."

I must confess that I have also experienced the immanentist weariness. Having started my literary research in the early nineteen seventies, I assimilated and practised the structuralist formalism then in vogue. There is no need for a recantation, however: there have been few advances in the development of a science that have favored getting to the core of its object of investigation as decisively as the methodology of intrinsic literary analysis. Having acknowledged this, I as well as other members of my generation must equally acknowledge the growing dissatisfaction that we felt when raising the question of the link between literary form and reality, a link which we as readers perceived with each new reading experience, but which our theoretical-critical perspective was unable to explain in a convincing manner. Moreover, sometimes we felt as if we were under a tacit agreement never to delve into this sibylline question, to which it was enough to oppose the sacrosanct axiom of the total autonomy of the literary work of art and the world created by it.

Beyond Genetic and Formal Realism

To sum up, I have so far considered two theoretical-critical modes of literary realism: a "conscientious" or "correspondence" realism, which I have labeled "genetic," and a "conscious" or "coherence" realism, which I have labeled "formal" or "immanent." As far as textual interpretation goes, the first kind leans toward "heteronomism" and the second kind toward "autonomism" (Leo H. Hoek 1981, 145–146). For genetic realism, a reality that precedes the work finds its transparent reflection within it through a literary art whose medium is paradoxically thin and self-effacing, being subordinated to the primary objective of recreating the external referent. For immanent or formal realism, by contrast, the only reality one can speak about is the one inherent in and simultaneous with the work itself, for it both originates and constitutes itself in this work *ex novo*.

I have found both theories to be unsatisfactory; they both lead to fallacies, although the immanentist fallacy is of primary concern here, if we are to reach an accurate and comprehensive understanding of the complex literary phenomenon. For, geneticism, strongly embedded in nineteenth-century critical-literary thought, seems already so far away from us and so thoroughly neutralized that the only dim possibility of its rebirth is in the form of a backlash against the excesses of formalism. The theoretical foundations of the latter are closer to us, and some of the fundamental traits of "postmodern" culture, such as the ludic and non-transcendent sense of creation, its metaliterary impulse, and so on, may still favor it.

New Perspectives

Assuming that the previous theoretical conjectures about literary realism have already been refuted, the time has now come, if we were to adopt Karl R. Popper's critical-rationalist vocabulary, to advance the process of understanding—always partial and relative—of truth, by perfecting the degree of knowledge already achieved through successive plausible conjectures that will in turn be subjected to rigorous critical proofs. But what conjecture shall we adopt next?

Let me first point out that the two concepts of realism already refuted are based on only two of the three elements of literary communication (the author, the message or the text, and the recipient). Thus, genetic realism relies exclusively on the relationship between the author and the world around him, which he apprehends through observation and mimetically reproduces as faithfully as possible. By contrast, formal realism relies solely on literariness: the work creates a textual reality, i.e., a reality disconnected from the referent. So we are left with the recipient's perspective, not as a possibility of escaping forward, but as a promising working hypothesis: centering the issue of literary realism on the reader, necessarily from the critic's or the researcher's perspective. Could we find here the point of equilibrium between alterity and immanence for which I pleaded earlier? I believe this is far from being a preposterous conjecture: in the reader, by the reader, and from the reader's standpoint, the universe of aesthetic forms is interwoven with that of human experience, considered both individually and socially.

Such a hypothesis would, moreover, find sufficient theoretical support in an "aesthetics of literary reception and response," which has flourished precisely in the wake of the relative exhaustion of various formalist structuralisms in the late 1960s and which grounds its methodological premises (going, of course, much further back than the sixties) in modern phenomenological thought. Additionally, studying how literature functions in relation to the reader raises a pragmatic question that involves both linguistics in general and semiotics in particular.

Modern phenomenology, as is well known, has developed mainly around one of Brentano's disciples, Edmund Husserl (1913, 1929, 1973), whose school includes Heidegger, but it also extends to other important figures of modern thought, such as Charles Sanders Peirce, one of the fathers of semiotics (who preferred calling it "phaneroscopy"). This philosophy, which is also a method, touches upon spheres as closely related to our central topic as the ontology of the real, the epistemology of perception (Maurice Merleau-Ponty 1945), Husserl's linguistic theory of signification as studied by Jacques Derrida (1967), as well as an aesthetics that includes Roman Ingarden's phenomenological theory of literature (1931, 1968). Given the importance of Ingarden's theory for an understanding of literary realism, I shall briefly summarize it, while also drawing the reader's attention to Javier San

Martín's excellent book (1986) on the phenomenological method in general.

For Ingarden, the literary work of art has its origin in the creative acts of the author's intentional consciousness. Its ontic foundation is of a physical nature—such as manuscript or printed paper, magnetic tape, computer disk, etc.—allowing it to endure through time, whereas its internal structure is a multilayered one. Thus, it consists of a layer of sounds and verbal constructions, a layer of semantic units, one of represented objectivities or intentional phrasal correlations, and finally, a layer of the schematic aspects under which these objectivities appear. The artistic intention creates a solid bond among all of the layers, justifying the polyphonic harmony of the work. Owing to its double linguistic layer (phonetic and semantic), moreover, the work is intersubjectively accessible and reproducible, so that it becomes an intentional intersubjective object that refers to an open—both spatially and temporally—community of readers. In this respect, the literary work of art is not a mere psychological phenomenon, for it transcends both the author's and the reader's conscious experiences.

But the literary work leaves many of its ontological elements in a potential state, because its entity is mainly a schematic one. Its active actualization on the part of the reader fills in some of the gaps of indeterminacy (Unbestimmtheitsstellen) or latent elements, and if this actualization is performed in a positive aesthetic spirit, it turns the artistic object that is the literary work into a fulfilled aesthetic object. In this respect, each of the layers that ontologically constitute the literary work requires different actualizations, but regardless of the concretization of the whole as a unit, one can single out, for the present purpose, the sense-giving process that the reader initiates at the level of the semantic units and represented objectivities—a task for which the schematic layer requires the contribution of the virtual or indeterminate elements, without which the work cannot attain its full existence. This opens a margin of variability between the artistic values inherent in the work itself and the aesthetic values reached through the concretization(s) that provide(s) the work with its complete ontological plenitude. The main difference between a literary work of art and its actualizations is, of course, that in the latter the potential elements are concretized and the gaps of indeterminacy filled. The artistic values belonging to different layers are some of those potential elements, and their aesthetic productivity largely depends on the system of relations that can be established between them, that is, on the qualitative harmony equivalent to the *Gestalt* or, in a different vocabulary, the structure.

For example, Roman Ingarden enumerates four different modes of cognition or apprehension of the literary work of art that correspond to the same number of epistemological alternatives and imply four different types of literary experience: a) the an-aesthetic or extra-aesthetic experience of a purely passive reader, uninterested in literature and having little literary "competence" as such; b) the purely intuitive aesthetic experience of the spontaneous and natural reader, the optimal recipient of the literary work of art; c) the "pre-aesthetic knowledge" of the work (Ingarden's term) resulting from an investigative attitude toward it; and d) the knowledge of an aesthetic concretization of the work resulting from the analysis of a full aesthetic experience of it.

So Ingarden's dialectic between the literary work as a schematic structure and its concretization in an aesthetic object can very well apply to the critical and theoretical problems of realism, providing a basic reference frame for a renewed understanding of this literary phenomenon. In a highly illuminating study, Michael Rifaterre (1979, 9) states that "le phénomène littéraire n'est pas seulement le texte, mais aussi son lecteur et l'ensemble des réactions possibles du lecteur au texte—énoncé et énonciation," with the help of which he proposes to move away from the kind of formalist immanentism that I also believe must be transcended if we are to rethink the issue of realism. Riffaterre refers to the understanding of literary acts in general, but what he says is equally valid for realism, containing several points quite pertinent to my own theoretical program: "ce phénomène se situe dans les rapports du texte et du lecteur, non du texte et de l'auteur, ou du texte et de la réalité. Par conséquent, contrairement à la tradition, qui aborde le texte de l'extérieur, l'approche de l'explication doit être calquée sur la démarche normale de la perception du message par son destinataire: elle doit aller de l'intérieur à l'extérieur" (1979, 27).

This has been the basic methodology of all the theoretical trends centered on the reader's perspective that have succeded both formalist immanentism and structuralism in Europe and the United States. One such trend is the so-called *Wirkungstheorie,* or theory of aesthetic response, which along with its complementary *Rezeptionstheorie,* or theory of literary reception, is the focus of the Konstanz School in Germany. The first of the two, as represented, among others, by Wolfgang Iser, fits my idea of realism better than the second. Its phenomenological foundation in Ingarden's work is obvious, and Iser relates it to a pragmatics that nowadays is largely in the vanguard of linguistics and semiotics. I am particularly interested in Iser's idea that, in the literary work of art, "the meaning must inevitably be pragmatic, in that it can never cover all the semantic potentials of the text, but can only open up one particular form of access to these potentials" (Iser 1976, 85). (For the relationship between concepts of literary meaning such as Iser's and the linguistic ideas of the later Wittgenstein, as well as those of Quine in particular, see Hilary Putnam 1983.)

In Iser's *Der Akt des Lesens,* we also read: "Meaning is no longer an object to be defined, but is an effect to be experienced" (1976, 10). So could we perhaps substitute here the word "realism" for "meaning"? And would we understand literary realism better if we regarded it as an effect or response, rather than as a mere copy or a purely immanent creation? In other words, could we speak of a realism that is never in essence, but always in act? There is another important point that Iser underscores: "Effects and responses are properties neither of the text nor of the reader; the text represents a potential effect that is realized in the reading process" (Iser 1976, IX). Therefore, when considering realism or any other literary issue, the perspective of the reader's response cannot exclude the formal or immanent one, which methodologically leaves us in a position of reasonable eclecticism—one of the most attractive features of both branches of the Konstanz School (the *Wirkungstheorie* continues the tradition of the intrinsic analysis of literature, whereas Jauss's *Rezeptionstheorie*, that of the extrinsic approaches to it).

There is nothing strange in this high regard for literary form if we recall the beginnings of Russian formalism, particularly those of the Moscow circle which became familiar with Husserl's *Logische Untersuchungen* through one of his disciples, Gustav Spet. Husserlian phenomenology also stands behind the literary theory of Czech formalism. For Mukařovsky, e.g., the literary work of art cannot be reduced to its material aspect—what he calls an "artifact"—but must be considered as an aesthetic object, that is, as an actualization of the "artifact" in the consciousness of the recipient, an idea remarkably similar to that of Ingarden's ontology of literature. Ingarden coincides with the formalists in granting priority, within his structural conception of the literary work, to the essentially verbal layers of this work, without belittling the importance of the reading process, or of the specific actualizations of the work's ontological plenitude.

Now I can fully outline the framework and scope of my research on literary realism, to which I shall apply the following Ingardenian phenomenological principles: 1) the principle of intentionality, deeply rooted in phenomenological philosophy, as applied to the literary act; 2) the principle of the literary work as a schematic formation and a layered structure, including a layer of represented objectivities; 3) the principle of the actualization of the literary work as a key element for its ontological plenitude, as well as its various actualizing modalities.

I shall also add a fourth principle, only implied by Ingarden, but recently incorporated successfully into the paradigm of the phenomenological understanding of literature—a principle that needs to be considered right away so that the other three can be harmonized with it. I am referring to the starting point of all phenomenology, which clearly shows Descartes's influence on Husserl: suspending belief in the reality of the natural world and thus bracketing, as it were, the inductions engendered by it. Through the "phenomenological reduction," as Husserl calls it, it becomes possible to reconsider all the contents of consciousness and to rely on the given, describing it in all its purity, according to the seminal motto of Husserlian philosophy: "Zu den Sachen selbst!" ("To the things themselves!"). (Especially illuminating in this regard is the second of the five lectures given by Husserl in Göttingen in April and May 1907, and first published in 1950).

Husserl himself identifies this principle with the *epoché* or the suspension of judgment advocated by the Greek New Academy and the Sceptics. Sextus Empiricus defined it as the state of mental rest by which we neither affirm nor deny. But, in literature, there is no better definition of it than what the Anglo-Saxon critics, citing Coleridge, call "the willing suspension of disbelief" (cf. Kendall L. Walton 1980). This phrase can be applied to the reader's attitude toward the literary work for which, as a rule, the fictional element is consubstantial. A literary reading would therefore constitute a true *epoché*, suspending the criterion of verifiability in regard to all the references to reality present in the text, as noted by Paul Ricoeur (1975, 266) and Dominique Combe (1985, 37).

Several other questions converge into the question of the literary *epoché* and deserve separate treatment. First, the fictional contract or pact itself, by which disbelief is suspended, involves the questions of play and convention, and especially that of their hermeneutic consequences. Secondly, there is the pragmatic question of defining the concrete "speech acts" characteristic of literary communication. And finally, there is the question (closely related to the previous ones) of the logical-semantic status of fictions or "fictionality."

The Sceptic and phenomenological origins of the literary *epoché* do not contradict the ludic component, to which I shall next turn. Indeed, ever since Plato (e.g., in *The Republic*, 602b; *The Sofist*, 234a–b; *Politics*, 288c; *Laws*, 796b, 899d–e), play has been considered fundamental for art, and particularly for imitation. In any case, it cannot be identified with arbitrariness and uselessness but, rather, with a self-transcending exercise, because artistic mimetic play expresses something other—more profound and committed—than what it seems to represent (*cf.* W. J. Verdenius 1949, 21–27).

Fiction As Play

The epistemological virtuality of play accounts for the growing interest that philosophy and science have shown in it since the second half of the nineteenth century—an issue that has been studied by Mihai I. Spariosu (1982). Prior to the nineteenth century, play in its double aspect of mundane attitude and a theoretical tool of mediation between inapprehensible reality and Reason, had already had an important part in Kant's philosophy. In a specifically artistic context, Schiller, in his letters on man's aesthetic education (*Über die ästhetische Erziehung des Menschen*, 1795) had completely identified art with play, and had further argued that "man does not play except when he is man in the fullest sense of the word, and he is not fully man except when he plays" (Letter XV).

It is true that today a ludic concept such as Schiller's will have its enemies. I am specifically referring to Georg Lukács who, in his *Aesthetics*, 1, 2 (1963, 9–10), even as he acknowledges, in Schiller's theory of play, "a deep humanism and, at the same time, a quite justified fear of the impact of capitalist production and division of labor on contemporary art," denounces it as "inevitably erroneous," "not only because—as has been repeatedly demonstrated—this doctrine makes the genesis of art—and therefore its essence—impossible, but also because Schiller's complete separation of art and artistic activity from labor, his coarse opposition between the two, must result in a drastic reduction of art, a loss of its content."

But Lukács's unfavorable view of the ludic is shared by few contemporary scholars, for nowadays one speaks of "play theory" (and an "aesthetics of science") in economics, cybernetics, statistics, political science, philosophy of science, and even in the experimental sciences, all of which have turned the ludic notion of *model* into a main theoretical tool. For example, Manfred Eigen, winner of the Nobel Prize for Chemistry in 1967, in a book written with Ruthild Winkler and entitled *Das Spiel: Naturgesetze steuern den Zufall* (Munich, 1975), imagines the universe as an endless game between chance events and natural laws (cf. Spariosu 1982, 33). Furthermore, Spariosu (1982, 32–33) notes: "The aesthetic attitude in modern science has also made possible the Einstenian revolution in physics, where the model (in this particular case Einstein's theory of relativity) no longer claims to disclose a certain (objective) reality, but rather, to *invent* it. This revolution, writes Herbert J. Muller, 'might be summarized as the triumph of the postulate over the axiom.'" Such developments are perfectly illustrated by Karl R. Popper's critical rationalism (not mentioned by Spariosu in this particular context), as opposed to scientific positivism. Further proof of the contemporary preference for the ludic model can be found in the interpretations of culture derived from Johan Huizinga's famous *Homo ludens* (Leiden, 1938), such as Roger Caillois's *Les jeux et les hommes* (Paris, 1958), as well as in Paul Feyerabend's "anarchist epistemology" (*Against Method*, London, 1975); Feyerabend also organizes the first volume of his *Philosophical Papers* around three basic ideas: criticism, proliferation of theories (or pluralism), and reality (Feyerabend 1981).

One of the clearest examples of the aesthetic and epistemological ramifications of the ludic concept is precisely the idea of *mimesis*, as well as that of the fictional pact or "suspension of disbelief"; moreover, as far as literary realism is concerned, I would argue, contrary to common opinion, that it is the realist mode, rather than the fantastic, that brings together the largest number of important elements linking the literary activity (as both diversion and revelation) with play.

In the field of literary semiology, Yuri Lotman is one of the most vigorous defenders of the impact of play on knowledge, through the construction of models that point unequivocally to reality (and in this he is followed closely by Jürgen Landwehr, 1975). For example, Lotman says: "A game is a model of a particular type of reality. It reproduces certain aspects of this reality, translating them into the language of its rules." The first of these rules is "the realization of a particular behavior—the 'ludic' one—different from practical behavior and determined by the use of scientific models" (Lotman 1970, 85). But this particular behavior, Lotman goes on to say, does not become displaced in the consciousness of the subject, who must simultaneously remember and not remember that he participates in a conventional situation. "The art of the game consists precisely in acquiring the habit of acting on a double plane" (Lotman 1970, 85), which frequently enables the player to discover his own profound nature (and Lotman illustrates his point by citing Rossellini's film, "General Della Rovere," which presents the case of a falsely assumed identity that becomes genuine in the end). "Anticipating a little," Lotman concludes, "we shall note that art even to a greater extent fulfils the same mission, which is fundamental to man" (1970, 86).

In turn, Rainer Warning, in an influential study of the pragmatics of literature as fictional discourse, considers the *faire semblant* characteristic of this discourse as essentially ludic, defining it "par la simultanéité de deux situations qui disposent chacune de son propre système déictique. Or, pour être présent dans deux situations simultanées, le sujet se soit confronté avec ces instructions contradictoires d'agir que la théorie de la communication appelle le paradoxe pragmatique du double-bind" (1979, 327–328). The double attitude characteristic of the literary *epoché* implies that, when reading an artistic—and therefore "fictional"—work, we may accept its assertions or judgments as true, even as we are fully aware of the *décalage* or the absolute genetic gap between these assertions and authentic reality. So the reader's acceptance of the fictional pact automatically conditions his hermeneutic attitude, play being the point of intersection between the two.

Also very significant, in this regard, is Hans Georg Gadamer's concept of *mimesis* as play and as a major cognitive operation, as well as the crucial role that he ascribes the ludic within his ontology of the art work and its hermeneutic significance, to which he devotes an entire chapter of *Wahrheit und Methode*. According to Gadamer, the *epoché* or fictional pact requires, on the one hand, the ludic act of suspending the rigorous rules of disbelief and verifiability; but, on the other hand, the same rigor that is voluntarily renounced operates in an immanent fashion within the game itself (the game of fiction, in our case): "Play fulfills its purpose only if the player loses himself in his play. It is not that relation to seriousness which directs us away from play, but only seriousness in playing makes the play wholly play" (Gadamer 1965, 92). Once the pact is accepted, the same modes of knowledge operate in the fictional hermeneutic process that Gadamer (1965, 7–10) mentions in regard to historical knowledge: trust in alien testimonies and self-conscious inference.

In Gadamer's view, "the work of art is not an object that stands over against a subject for itself" (1965, 145). In this sense, one must acknowledge the primacy of the game over the player's consciousness: "all playing is a being-played. The attraction of a game, the fascination it exerts, consists precisely in the fact that the game tends to master the players" (1965, 95). But it is in art that play reaches its most exigent and perfect expression, transforming itself into what Gadamer calls *Gebilde*: an entirely completed or established structure or construction, through which art "has found its measure in itself and measures itself by nothing outside it" (1965, 101), being oriented toward truth. The world of the art work "is in fact a wholly transformed world. By means of it everyone recognizes that that is how things are" (1965, 102). Gadamer contrasts the artistic universe with reality *tout court*, which he defines as "what is untransformed." For him, art is precisely "the raising of this reality into its truth" (1965, 102).

In turn, according to Gadamer, the cognitive significance of *mimesis*, which lies at the foundation of all artistic expression, resides in recognition. And what he has to say about recognition will help us understand the epistemological background of realism even better than before: "The joy of recognition is . . . that more becomes known than is already known. In recognition, what we already know emerges, as if through an illumination, from all the chance and variable circumstances that condition it and is grasped in its essence. It is known as something" (1965, 102).

Equally important to our theory of literary realism is Wittgenstein's application of the ludic concept to the process of linguistic communication in his *Philosophische Untersuchungen* (1953)—one of the fundamental texts of analytic philosophy and modern pragmatics. Wittgenstein (1953, 7) uses the term "language game" for the totality of language, as well as for each and every discrete act related to it (cf. Wittgenstein 1953, 23–25; and also Brand 1975, 115–133, particularly 131–132). "Language game" is in fact a very appropriate metaphor, because every linguistic event occurs according to certain rules and through a specific competence referring to those rules. For Wittgenstein (1953, 40–41), inventing and reading a story is, of course, one of the "language games" ("Eine Geschichte erfinden; und lesen," 1953, 23); but here, in order to confine ourselves to the literary *epoché* or fictional pact as it relates to literary realism, we shall single out Wittgenstein's principle (1953, 43) that completely integrates his semantics and pragmatics. This principle says that if the meaning of a word depends on its use in language ("Die Bedeutung eines Wortes ist sein Gebrauch in der Sprache," 1953, 60), then one must reject the existence of essential meanings and accept only the kind that can be explained by means of—and starting from—certain "language games" (1953, 77). This principle is systematically developed by "speech act" theory, which I shall soon examine. Translated into our field of research, it represents a rejection of what I have called "genetic realism" and have related to the "propositional phantom" of Wittgenstein's *Tractatus Logico-Philosophicus*. If there is no essential meaning, one can no longer accept a realism of essences, and, consequently, one will have to turn to a realism "in act," explained in phenomenological and pragmatic terms. My next chapter will attempt precisely this kind of explanation.

3

Phenomenology and Pragmatics of Realism

As Victoria Camps points out in an excellent study of the philosophical and ethical aspects of linguistic pragmatics, the later Wittgenstein "gives language an autonomy in relation to reality and 'dissolves' the problems raised by the 'referential' theories of meaning" (1976, 79). Against a pure linguistic competence, moreover, Wittgenstein postulates a pragmatic competence by which the listener "must be able to understand the intention of the speaker, and capture what the speaker, following the appropriate conventions, 'wishes to tell him' really" (Camps 1976, 80). Such views favor an interpretation of literary realism primarily from the perspective of the reader. But, even more concretely, the last quotation mentions two basic aspects of our problematic: intentionality and convention.

Intentionality

I have already identified Husserl's concept of intentionality as crucial for a phenomenological theory of literary realism. To this we can now add P. H. Grice's thesis (1969, 251–259) that the intention of the speaker (S) to produce, with X (an occasional rather than a natural meaning), a certain effect (E) in the listener (L), making L recognize the intention of S, is, therefore, an intention that transcends the purely individual and becomes intersubjective. So it is the intersubjective character of phenomenological intentionality that is important in the present context.

The growing influence of pragmatic perspectives has contributed to an increased use of the concept of intention in the field of linguistics—as John R. Searle's well-known book (1983) testifies—a development that was already present in the field of literary theory and criticism more than forty years ago. Witness, for instance, Alfonso Reyes's critical writings of that period, which had a definite phenomenological orientation: in a 1940 article, later included in his volume *La experiencia literaria* (1942), Reyes rather faithfully develops some of Husserl's ideas on the dichotomy between reality and fiction (which we shall explore later on), concluding with the following statement: "The historian attempts to capture a specific real individual; the novelist, a human model, whether possible or impossible. The emphasis on intention can never be strong enough" (1942, 71).

During the same period, although with much less philosophical rigor, William K. Wimsatt and Monroe Beardsley coined their term "intentional fallacy" as a successful battle cry of immanentist criticism against its genetic counterpart—a fallacy that identifies the author's purpose with the objective value of the literary work. Revising his views in 1968, Wimsatt came upon a notion deeply rooted in the phenomenological tradition that he had not considered before, namely, the notion of shared intentionality or co-intentionality: "an art work is something which emerges from the private, individual, dynamic, and intentionalistic realm of its maker's mind and personality; it is in a sense (and this is especially true of the verbal work of art) made of intentions or intentionalistic material. But at the same time, in the moment it emerges, it enters a public and in a certain clear sense an objective realm; it claims and gets attention from an audience; it invites and receives discussion, about its meaning and value, in an idiom of inter-subjectivity and conceptualization" (Wimsatt 1968, 194). In this respect, I agree with Ralph Freedmann (1976, 157) that it was phenomenological criticism that contributed the most to solving the problem of the poem's formalist isolation from life, without renouncing the autonomy of the poetic text, a problem in which the concept of intentionality plays an important role.

As John D. Boyd (1968, 63) reminds us in his book on the function of mimesis, the concept of intentionality, which

Husserl takes over from his master Brentano and which can also be found in Heidegger, Sartre, and Merleau-Ponty among others, has a long tradition in Thomist thought up to Jacques Maritain, but assumes a decidedly Cartesian shade with Husserl. Thus, in Husserl's *Ideen* (1913, 106), we read: *"Against the thesis of the world, which is a "contingent" one, there stands the thesis of my pure I and of the life of this I, which is a "necessary" thesis,* an absolutely indubitable one. *Not all things given in the person may exist. No experience given in the person may not exist*: such is the essential law that defines this necessity and that contingency." In other words, for Husserl the Kantian distinction between "noumenon" (what is in the subject) and "phenomenon" (what is not in the subject) is invalid. There are no things in themselves: there is only being that can be known—a thesis whose relevance for a phenomenological theory of literary realism can hardly be ignored. D. Souché-Dagues reformulates this thesis well in a monograph on the develpment of the concept of intentionality in Husserlian phenomenology: "ce n'est désormais ni le *Je suis* ni '*le monde est*' que peuvent réprésenter le point de départ authentique d'une ontologie phénoménologique, mais plutôt le: *Je suis-le monde est,* c'est-à-dire le thème de la corrélation intentionnelle au sein de toute expérience. C'est bien donc l'intentionnalité qui devienne le fil directeur de la pensée, c'est-à-dire de la pensée de l'être" (1972, 240).

Phenomenology in fact studies life experiences (*Erlebnisse*) that are intentional insofar as they point toward an object which may or may not be real, but which, as an unavoidable reference, is in any case a constitutive part of intentional life experience and, therefore, is also studied by it. In Husserl's fourth lecture (1950, 67) we read: "Cognitive experiences—and this is something that belongs to their essence—have an *intentio*; they mention something; they refer, in one way or another, to an object. It is their duty to refer to an object, even though the object does not belong to them." The nature of the object of the life experience or the intentional act is indifferent to the criterion of reality, which introduces a highly relevant element for the understanding of literary phenomena: "The act that 'lacks an object' (*Gegenstandslosigkeit*) essentially remains, of course, an intentional reference to an object: it is just that the object it refers to does not exist" (Husserl 1973, 39n).

According to Husserl, then, intentionality is the activity that moves from the cognitive I to the transcendental phenomenon in order to give it a meaning. But this phenomenon can be both a reality and a simulacrum, in the same manner in which, according to Gilbert Durand (1964, 88), consciousness can imagine the world in two ways. One is a direct way, in which the thing itself seems to rise before the mind, the other is an indirect one: "Dans tous ces cas de conscience indirecte, l'objet absent est réprésenté à la conscience par une *image*, au sens très large de ce terme." And Durand concludes: "A vrai dire la différence entre pensée directe et pensée indirecte n'est pas aussi tranchée que nous venons, par souci de clarté, de exposer. Il vaudrait mieux écrire que la conscience dispose de différents degrés de l'image . . . dont les deux extrèmes seraient constitués par l'adéquation totale, la présence perceptive, ou l'inadéquation la plus poussée" (1964, 88). In turn, Morse Peckham, in an essay provocatively entitled "Is the Problem of Literary Realism a Pseudo-Problem?" (1970, 98), considers that things are immediate signs which, when artistically imitated, produce other, mediated signs.

Reality as a conglomerate of perceptible and perceived phenomena acquires meaning through an act of understanding or intentional life-experience. So we can ask ourselves: what acts comparable to intentional life-experiences can be found in the literary communicative process? We can undoubtedly distinguish at least three: the apprehension of the world by the writer, the production of the text, and the reading of this text by its addressee. And as every intentional act constructs intentional objects, we could speak of a reality perceived by the author, of a literary work of art created by him, and of a world projected by the reader, starting from this work.

We can bring the phenomenological theme of intentionality closer to the concerns of literary realism by organizing it around three concepts: imagination, symbol, and meaning. The relationship between intentionality and the imagination is obvious: "The intention of a text is realized in the reader's imagination," as Wolfgang Iser (1975b, 34) notes. Here, in addition to Gilbert Durand's *L'imagination symbolique*, one should mention Jean Paul Sartre's treatise on *L'imaginaire*, the phenomenological orientation of which is evident from the subtitle: *Psychologie phénoménologique de l'imagination*. For Sartre, "l'intention est au centre de la conscience: c'est elle qui vise l'objet, c'est-à-dire qui le constitue pour ce qu'il est" (Sartre 1940, 27); furthermore, "l'imagination n'est pas un pouvoir empirique et surajouté de la conscience, c'est la conscience tout entière en tant qu'elle réalise" (1940, 358). And since the cognitive I does not distinguish between a world of images and a world of objects, "les deux mondes, l'imaginaire et le réel, sont constitués par les mêmes objets; seuls le groupement et l'interprétation de ces objets varient. Ce qui définit le monde imaginaire comme l'univers réel, c'est une attitude de la conscience" (1940, 45–46).

These last observations are highly pertinent to a phenomenological theory of realism. And so is Sartre's occasional pragmatic emphasis: "la conscience imageante que nous produisons devant une photographie est un acte. . . . Nous avons conscience, en quelque sorte, *d'animer* la photo, de lui prêter sa vie pour en faire une image" (1940, 44–45). If we substitute, in this passage, a literary work for the photograph, we have an exact description of the working of the reader's imagination in realist literature. Sartre reminds us that for Husserl the image was a "remplissement" (*Erfüllung*) of signification, and he adds that "c'est l'intention" (1940, 64) which constitutes the image and fills in all the fadings and instabilities of perception.

In this context, Sartre makes an interesting comparison between two essentially literary intentional life-experiences, that of the reader of a novel and and that of the theater-goer, in terms similar to Roman Ingarden's description of the stage as a limit case of literary ontology (Ingarden 1931, § 57). Thus Sartre writes: "En réalité dans la lecture comme au théâtre, nous sommes en présence d'un monde et nous attribuons à ce monde juste autant d'existence qu'à celui du théâtre; c'est-à-dire une existence complète dans l'irréel," so that "assister à une pièce de théâtre, c'est appréhender *sur* les acteurs, les personnages, sur les arbres de carton la forêt de *As you like it*. Lire, c'est réaliser *sur* les signes le contact avec le monde irréel" (Sartre 1940, 127, 129). In phenomenological terms, this means projecting intentional objectivities corresponding to characters, their environment and moments, actions and words, starting from mere verbal signs in the case of the novel, or, in the case of the theater, from signs belonging to different codes and real objectivities, such as actors, stage props, stage space—mentioned in the "secondary text" of stage directions—the effective corporeality of which does not lead us to misunderstand their condition of pure dramatic signs on the stage.

The semiotic implications of phenomenology are crucial, not only in regard to Peirce, but also to Husserl himself, as Derrida demonstrates in *La voix et le phénomène* (1967), where he insists, as we have seen, on the concept of intersubjective intentionality or co-intentionality. In the first of his *Logische Untersuchungen* focusing on expression and signification, Husserl argues that the communicative process occurs "because the listener understands the intention of the speaker. . . . What enables spiritual commerce and makes the discourse between two people be a discourse, is the correlation established by the physical side of the discourse between the mutually implied physical and psychic life-experiences that people experience through this commerce. Speaking and hearing, transmitting psychic experiences by means of the word and taking them in through audition, find themselves in mutual coordination" (Husserl 1929, 240 § 7). Although the type of communication to which Husserl refers is very different from literary communication, it is nevertheless important for our theory of realism to retain the phenomenological idea of intersubjective intentionality or co-intentionality.

For example, S. Y. Kuroda (1976, 126) assumes with Husserl that "the essence of linguistic performance consists in meaning-assigning acts (*Bedeutungsverleihende Akt*) and meaning-fulfilling acts (*Bedeutungserfüllende Akt*)," and that, phenomenologically speaking, *meaning* is "an intentional object" (1976, 130). So even though "the meaning-realizing act" will take place "in both the author's and the reader's consciousness" (1976, 137), phenomenological co-intentionality will never fall into Wimsatt and Beardsley's fallacy by confusing what is proper to the author with what is proper to the reader, because the two come into contact only through the text, and so there can be no identity of contexts (a situation more common than its opposite). One need not proscribe some readers' desire of reconstructing the author's intention, as discussed by Stanley E. Fish (1976, 476). Rather, one should remember that "in addition to the author's intentions for his work, and the (supposed) 'intention' of the work itself, there are also the phenomenological 'intentions' of the reader towards the work—that is, the reader's own generative perceptions of the work" (Hancher 1972, 851).

As far as conventions go, it is obvious that one must resort to them in order to communicate an intention intersubjectively, and the realist intention is no exception to this rule. Apart from the fact that reality itself largely results from social conventions, the fictional *epoché* is equally a conventional complex. This complex has been studied by Ada Wildekamp, Ineke van Montfort, and William van Ruiswijk, who conclude: "'Fictionality' is to be considered as a relative and, by and large, conventionally determined phenomenon that presents itself in the actual communication situation under the influence of the situational conditions of production and reception in connection with possible textual indicators" (1980, 554). Hence the accuracy of Rainer Warning's assertion (1979, 331) that fictionality is essentially *contractual*.

Here we have already entered the domain of the second type of questions to which I assumed the fictional contract or pact as *epoché* would lead us in our search for new theoretical perspectives on literary realism: the more specifically linguistic pragmatics of speech-act theory. In this context, the fictional pact implies renouncing the principle of verifiability (cf. Anderegg 1973). Fictional utterances are illocutionary acts of assertion without verification, which is one of the propriety rules of this type of act. Moreover, they are not bound by the sincerity rule proper to normal acts (a rule that, as we

have seen, the theorists and the practicioners of genetic realism have invoked in flagrant violation of the very essence of
literary discourse).

The Acts of Fiction

Richard Ohmann (1971) is one of the first critics to have
raised this pragmatic issue in the context of a definition of
literature. He concludes that literary discourse lacks real illocutionary power, possessing it only in a "mimetic" manner, by
which he means intentionally mimetic: "Specifically, a literary work *purportedly* imitates (or reports) a series of speech
acts, which in fact have no other existence. By doing so, it
leads the reader to imagine a speaker, a situation, a set of ancil-
lary events, and so on" (1971, 14); which means, by a twist
especially convenient for our pragmatic theory of realism, that
fiction involves not only the Aristotelian *mimesis* of actions
or of the external referent, but also this other *mimesis* of
speech acts. Further useful elements of Ohmann's pragmatic
definition of literature (1971, 17–18) include: 1) "A literary
work creates a 'world'"—we shall return later to this theme,
already present in Gadamer; 2) "Literature is autonomous" in
relation to the outside world; and 3) "Literature is play,"
because through it we become *accomplices* rather than *col-
laborators* of the author-transmitter (cf. also Lázaro Carreter
1980, 203).

In turn, for J. R. Searle (1975) the illocutionary speech
act of "narrating a fiction" does not constitute a specific
entity. Iris Murdoch, or any other author, upon writing the
first narrative sentence in one of her stories "is pretending,
one could say, to make an assertion, or acting as if she were
making an assertion, or going through the motions of making an assertion, or imitating the making of an assertion"
(Searle 1975, 324). In Searle's description of the nature of the
literary text, *"pretend is an intentional verb"* (1975, 325), and
the whole process is possible because of the existence of *ad
hoc* conventions, so that Searle concludes: "in this sense, to
use Wittgenstein jargon, telling stories really is a separate language game" (1975, 326).

As one can see, there are no substantial differences between Ohmann's and Searle's interpretations. In turn, Gottfried Gabriel borrows an expression from Searle to characterize fictional discourse in terms of "speaking *as if*," because the literary transmitter acts *as if* he were speaking about a specific referent that does not exist, and *as if* he were performing a particular speech act, which he is not, because, in his case, "the rules of reference . . . denotation . . . sincerity, argumentation, and consequence are out of place" (Gabriel 1979, 246–249). Samuel R. Levin, in his insightful contribution to the subject (1976), does not contradict these interpretations, but adds to them a nuance of his own: instead of the deep structure that normally introduces a true or fictive assertion of the type "I say to you," in literary discourse there operates another "higher implicit sentence": "I imagine my self in and invite you to conceive a world in which . . ." (1976, 150). And just as Searle specifies that his "pretend" is an *intentional* verb, Levin warns that his "invite" is a "performative" one (1976, 152), opening the way for the addressee's acceptance or rejection of a pact and, subsequently (if the pact is accepted), for a vast protocol of intersubjective intentionalities.

More recently, Gérard Genette (1991, 41) speaks explicitly of "acts of fiction" when referring to narrative literary assertions from a linguistic standpoint. Going against Searle's thesis, Genette believes that these acts of fiction are not feigned assertions, but must be placed among what Searle calls *declarative* speech acts, in which the utterance, by virtue of the institutional authority conferred upon its subject, exerts a certain power over reality. One can relate Genette's view to the narrative pact, with its "voluntary suspension of disbelief" by which we, the readers, acknowledge the literary narrator's ability to *institute* a world, the rules of which we accept just as we do those of a game. An assertion about reality made by, say, a historical or a scientific text, institutes an objective state of affairs, whereas a fictive assertion institutes a "mental state" appropriate for "possible worlds," which Genette does not mention explicitly, but to the semantics of which I shall turn presently. Genette does, however, mention the marked *intentional* character of such linguistic processes, insofar as their

success largely depends on "faire reconnaître son intention fictionnelle": "un acte de fiction peut échouer comme tel parce que son destinataire n'a pas perçu sa fictionalité, comme don Quichotte montant sur les tréteaux de maître Pierre pour estourbir les méchants et sauver les gentils" (Genette 1991, 60).

Félix Martínez Bonati's earlier article on the act of fiction writing (1978) also deals with intersubjective intentionality and related issues, coming close to my own pragmatic view of literary realism. Relying on his own experience as a reader, the Chilean critic refuses to consider fictive propositions as semi-assertions or quasi-judgements. The latter term, *Quasi-Urteile*, is used by Roman Ingarden (1931, § 25a, "Gibt es keine Quasi-Urteile im literarischen Kunstwerk?") to describe the assertions that appear in a literary work, and Frege, Austin, and Searle, among others, coincide with him (Sartre, in his phenomenology of the imagination, also speaks of *assertions imageantes*, 1940, 188).

Martínez Bonati bases his position on the fact that an effective creation of the world proposed by the literary work requires the total effectiveness of such assertions. Consequently, the literary *epoché* with its subsequent fictional pact "does not mean accepting a fictitious image of the world, but, prior to that, accepting a fictitious discourse. Mark well: not the author's feigned or incomplete one, but a complete and authentic discourse, even though fictitious, of the *Other*, of a source of language . . . which is not the author, and since it is a source proper to a fictitious discourse, it is also fictitious or simply imaginary" (1978, 142). Martínez Bonati's view is equally shared by Susana Reisz de Rivarola (1979, 103–104) and later on by J.-K. Adams, for whom the principal convention operating in fictional discourse is that of the writer attributing his assertions to another speaker, "which means, the writer attributes the performance of his speech acts to a speaker he creates" (Adams 1985, 10).

By insisting on the reader's perspective, Martínez Bonati's study has contributed a fundamental element, somewhat neglected in other contributions based on pragmatic linguistic theories. For example, Jürgen Landwehr (1975, 181), upon failing to detect any distinguishing semantic or syntactic marks of fictionality, concludes that it is a category constituted pragmatically (see also Siegfried J. Schmidt 1980b, 528–529). For Landwehr, therefore, the fictional text results from the intentional modifications performed by the agents—transmitter and recipient—of the act of communication. When both agents perform the same modification, the fictionality of the text will become complete as co-intentional, but it is sufficient that one of them perform it for the text to become fictional as a whole.

Yet I believe that Landwehr's sufficient condition of intentional modification applies only in the case of the recipient, never in the case of the transmitter. In this respect I also disgree with J.-K. Adams (1985, 9), who argues that the writer-transmitter is the only one to enjoy the prerogative of deciding whether his text will be fictional or not and, subsequently, of creating a differentiated pragmatic structure to support his decision. To me, however, the pragmatic nature of Adams's argument results in a self-contradiction, because the literary structure of which he speaks will necessarily be actualized according to its user's or reader's specific intention, even if one rightly confers on this structure a certain ability to condition (rather than determine) its own reception. If the contemporary notion of literariness depends on the reader's reception of and response to texts, the same holds true regarding the fictionality of these texts. That the author has conceived of them as fictional is not decisive: they can in fact be read as true, because it is solely up to the reader to grant them such status. Landwehr, then, should speak only of two, rather than three, possibilities of intentional modification: the co-intentional—certainly the more common of the two—and the purely intentional, on the part of the recipient. (I shall later apply this idea specifically to my phenomenological and pragmatic theory of realism.)

In the background of the foregoing linguistic considerations there lies the third issue implied in the literary *epoché*, which is as closely linked to the pragmatic theories of speech or language acts as the other two. I am referring to the logical-semantic status of fiction, to be distinguished from the clear-cut binary opposition of truth and falsehood. Indeed, the issue of fictionality has lately elicited a great deal of interest among scholars of formal logic and philosophical semantics. They have, moreover, been joined by those who approach literature from the fields of sociology, psychology, history, and—naturally—linguistics, in order to develop different aspects of their own disciplines. The literary phenomenon equally provides "a severe testing ground for formal semantics," as Richard Routley (1979, 3–30) notes in his introduction to an issue of *Poetics* devoted to the logic of fiction, and many studies on this topic have recently appeared in such purely philosophical journals as *American Philosophical Quarterly, Synthèse, Philosophia, The Journal of Aesthetics and Art Criticism, The Journal of Philosophy, The Philosophical Review*, etc. This is, then, a common ground for logicians, linguists, language philosophers, and literary theorists alike, as Jens F. Ihwe and Hannes Rieser point out in the same issue of *Poetics* (1979, 63–84), but starting from different intellectual and methodological presuppositions—we should not forget that the perspective of artistic literariness is glaringly absent from practically all of the approaches to fictionality that come from fields other than literary science, since these approaches are naturally guided by investigative interests different from ours.

I do not wish to imply, however, that we cannot use the advances of semantic logic in the study of the fictive in order to cast light upon certain aspects of the theory of realism. For example, I consider the so-called "possible world semantics," developed by Woods, Pavel, Chateaux, Heintz, among others, to be particularly illuminating in this respect. Its philosophical foundations obviously originate in Leibnitz's thought, which J. J. Bodmer and J. J. Breitinger had already applied to literary criticism in their *Kritische Dichtkunst* (1740); their pioneering efforts, however, were not immediately followed up.

"Possible Worlds" Semantics

It is important, therefore, to begin by establishing the fundamental difference between Leibnitz's metaphysics and its present-day semantic derivative. For Leibnitz, imaginary

worlds are but imitations of possible worlds that are meta-
physically given but lacking in actualization, whereas the contemporary theory—as Lubomir Doležel (1985, 81) has well
argued in a fine article on Kafka—develops a radically non-
mimetic, constructivist semantics of possible and fictional
worlds. Furthermore, in Husserl one can find a very similar
perspective, which Anna-Teresa Tyminiecka (1983) has
adopted in studying a "phenomenological conception of possible worlds."

In addition to the world empirically observed, or the
"actual world," there are other possibilities created by the
human mind, thought, imagination, language, and additional
semiotic activities. In the first type of world, in order to prove
linguistic assertions as such, one has to conform entirely to
the principle of correspondence with reality (Alfred Tarski
1944), whereas in the second types one can accept what
Thomas G. Pavel (1976) calls "ersatz-sentences," or "sentences
of substitution" that can be evaluated only in relation to the
possible or fictional world to which they refer. They are true if
they conform to the rules proposed, and false if they fail to
do so.

"Possible worlds" semantics finds most of its applications in the artistic and literary domain, or in what Wolterstoff
(1979) calls "worlds of work of art," Howell (1979), "worlds of
imagination," Doležel (1979), "narrative worlds," and Routley
(1979), "fictional worlds," although not exclusively in them.
At the beginning of this century, Hans Vaihinger (1911) had
already noted that science, philosophy, law, etc., employed
certain fictions that, without referring to anything empirically
objectifiable, could not be considered false. They do not transcribe anything from reality, but they help understand it
within the scope of an intellectual construction. They are very
much like literary creations, which Frank Kermode (1966,
54–55) in turn identifies with what Vaihinger calls "consciously false fictions" of extraordinary heuristic value (cf.
also Roy Pascal 1977).

Linking "possible worlds" semantics with speech-act theory, Lubomir Doležel (1980, 11–12) proposes the principle of
"authenticating authority" as one of the basic modes of con-

structing a narrative fiction, which is a very common type of "possible world." For Doležel, this principle has an illocutionary force of a special nature, similar to performative speech acts and easily applicable to Gérard Genette's theory of acts of fiction. Doležel's analogy is based on the fact that "the performative illocutionary force is carried only by speech acts uttered by speakers who have the necessary authority." Authority would thus provide the key to these possible worlds, so that what Doležel calls "fictional truth" would strictly be "'truth in/of' the constructed narrative world," always conforming to the criterion of the "agreement or disagreement with authenticated narrative facts" (1980, 15).

Doležel's thesis (and to a large extent Genette's) can be paraphrased as follows: the "possible worlds" constructed by literary narratives are systems of fictitious facts created by speech acts that proceed from an authoritative source. This source can be found literally in the enunciating instance constituted by the fictional complex of *implicit author* and *narrator* (or narrators), and, at the empirical level, by the writer who, according to Cesare Segre (1978, 179), "si arroga insomma el diritto di *instaurazione* di mondi possibili, si attribuisce, su questi mondi, *l'omniscenza* ed esercita . . . una *selezione* di carattere funzionale." Segre, moreover, citing the passages in Aristotle's *Poetics* and in Ludovico Castelvetro's Commentary to it that deal with verisimilitude, argues that since a literary work builds a "possible world" different from that of empirical experience, everything that subjects itself to the laws of immanent coherence generated by it becomes verisimilar. Finally, one can define a fictional world as one which, in Richard Routley's words (1979, 7), is "authored and which satisfies structural requirements."

Realism, Reference, and Meaning

"Possible worlds" semantics contains a limitation that diminishes its usefulness in understanding literary realism. The autonomous and immanent character of the possible world created by fictional discourse according to the rules just mentioned places us completely within the realm of intensional semantics; this semantics deals more with the game of expressive forms than with the referential relation—a fact that Doležel (1980, 24) does not ignore—and thus it can easily make us slide back into formal or immanent realism. Of course, I have already expressed my dissatisfaction with the formal approach and have argued that it is not a matter of re-embracing the opposite fallacy of genetic realism, but rather of finding the point of equilibrium between the autonomy of the created world and its undeniable referential function. Jens F. Ihwe and Hannes Rieser (1979, 77) have equally deplored the fact that "in most discussions about the application of possible world semantics" the extensional aspects remain "completely neglected."

What can be of great help here is Gottlob Frege's theory of meaning in the natural languages (1892, 25–50), which draws a distinction between *Bedeutung,* or the referential object of a sign, and *Sinn,* or its sense (the manner in which the linguistic expression designates this object, or the information it provides about it so that it can be identified). Frege's opposition of *Sinn* and *Bedeutung* is commonly related to Carnap's opposition of "extensional" and "intensional," or Quine's theories of "reference" and "meaning." We could extend the parallel all the way to Michael Riffaterre's *signification/ significance* (in Barthes et al. 1982, 93–94), but equal attention should be paid to its affinity with Husserl's phenomenological theory of language in the first of his *Logische Untersuchungen* (§ 12 a 16), as studied by Derrida (1967). In the wake of Frege, Husserl (1929, 248–258) also makes a distinction between the object (*Gegenstand*), or the non-verbal phenomenon denoted by the word, and meaning *(Bedeutung),* or the manner in which the object is presented (thus using the term *Bedeutung* in an opposite sense from that of Frege). Finally, as is well known, Charles W. Morris has also employed Frege's dichotomy in order to expand his semiotic scheme by distinguishing between *semantics* proper, which concerns itself with the relations between signs and their mental representations, and *sigmatics,* which concerns itself with the relations between signs and the objects they refer to.

So the question of fictionality, and therefore that of realism, cannot be solved only on the basis of semantics (cf.

Walter Mignolo 1982, 223–224) but also, and perhaps preferably, on the basis of sigmatics; in turn, this sigmatics should
become part of pragmatics, as argued by Leo H. Hoek, one of
its strongest defenders along with G. Klaus. For, according to
Hoek, pragmatics "réprésente le point de vue le plus large,
celui qui est en dernière instance déterminant du sens de
l'énoncé et donc celui où devrait commencer toute réflexion
sémiotique" (1981, 34). I have come to the same conclusion
when referring to Ludwig Wittgenstein's shift in his views of
the relation between language and the world.

The need to move from a pure "possible worlds" semantics to a new sigmatics and/or pragmatics of fictionality and
realism is excellently illustrated by Ziva Ben-Porat's study on
"Represented Reality and Literary Models. European Autumn
on Israeli Soil" (1986). Although Ben-Porat does not consciously employ sigmatics as a theoretical tool (in fact, she
does not even mention the term), she nevertheless practices it
implicitly in her exploration of the theme of autumn in modern Hebrew poetry.

From a semantic perspective, the representations of
autumn in the texts that Ben-Porat analyzes are totally coherent, since the different poetic motifs employed agree with the
internal logic that informs the autonomous fictional world.
These representations, moreover, conform to models that are
well established, i.e., conventionalized, in the literary tradition, in which the theme of autumn, starting with the descriptive motif of the falling of leaves and the general retreat of
nature, is metaphorically related to the theme of destruction
and death. But in sigmatic—or simply pragmatic—terms, the
phenomenon is surprising, if not contradictory. Because of
geographical reasons, an Israeli reader lives a "reality-base"
in which the initial motif—exfoliation—does not occur as an
objective referent. In principle, this has no derogatory implications for the poems studied by Ziva Ben-Porat; it simply
means, according to her, that "the European concepts of
autumn have then superimposed upon the Israeli reality-base,"
for, after fifty years of existence, modern Hebrew-Israeli poetry
remains "a subsystem within the European literary system
and because of its unique history, is a dependent one in many

respects" (1986, 56–57); so much so that, even though their reality-bases are totally different, the two literary systems share the same models or conventional repertoires of representation.

Ben-Porat even goes so far as to assert that a Hebrew poem faithful to the autumn reality of its territory "will not be generally recognized as a seasonal poem" (1986, 97), an assertion also supported by the fact that the Israeli popular songs on the same theme use the repertoire based on the European tradition. The particular historical circumstances of Israeli literature can perfectly well explain this contradiction. Both the Israeli poets and their readers have been shaped by a Western European literary tradition and have lived for some time in the geographical environment informing that tradition. Only time will tell whether they will continue to find this contradiction acceptable, or whether the internal—or intensional—world of the poem will end up adjusting to the external—or extensional—world of the writer and the reader.

As a purely theoretical consideration, G. Ephraim Lessing had already discovered, in his *Laokoon* (1766), the utopian character of a descriptive poetry such as Albrecht von Heller's *Alpen*, from which he selects a few passages enumerating plants and flowers to comment upon (1977, 176–179). The impossibility of such a descriptive project lies less in the reader's not having previously experienced the reality of what the poet wishes to paint with words than in the radical ontological difference between the marked spatial dimension of the visual arts and the continuous movement of temporal arts such as literature. It is, therefore, the impossibility of offering a global, stabilized vision, a panorama filled with shapes and colors—rather than the reader's lack of prior knowledge—that constitutes the major difficulty, because, as Lessing points out elsewhere in his *Laokoon*, what we find pleasant in art is not what our eyes see, but rather what our imagination discovers to be pleasant through them.

So, in order to overcome semantic reductionism, we must sigmatically play with the orders of both *Sinn* and *Bedeutung* at the same time. Siegfried J. Schmidt (1976, 165) underscores this fact when he states that a literary text "constitutes a 'world' . . . or a system of worlds . . . which is (or can be) related to other worlds/world systems . . . constituted by other texts, or *to our normal world system of experience EW*, in our present society, at a certain time" (my emphasis). Along the same lines, Lubomir Doležel (1979, 24) acknowledges an "intensional narrative world" defined as "the prime target of semantic interpretation," as well as its "derived 'background'" or "extensional primary narrative world." And, from the standpoint of a phenomenological hermeneutics, Paul Ricoeur (1983, 117–118) speaks of an *intersection* between the world of the text and that of the listener or the reader: "Ce qui est communiqué, en dernière instance, c'est, par delà le sens d'une oeuvre, le monde qu'elle projette et qui en constitue l'horizon. En ce sens, l'auditeur ou le lecteur le reçoivent selon leur propre capacité d'accueil qui, elle aussi, se définit par une situation à la fois limitée et ouverte sur un horizon de monde."

In this respect, I find it difficult to accept the way in which Tomás Albaladejo (1986, 124–125) applies "possible worlds" semantics to the short novels of Leopoldo Alas ("Clarín"), because he places these novels in an entirely intensional plane. For example, Albaladejo says: "The system of worlds in the narrative text is constituted by the worlds of the various characters and, therefore, by the subworlds within each of these worlds, as well as by the relations between the subworlds of various worlds, and among the different subworlds of a text globally considered." But the truly operative dimension of "possible worlds" semantics should be the extensional one, by means of which a dialectical relation between the author's and the reader's (rather than the characters') respective world or worlds is established through the text.

This last view is supported by Benjamin Harshaw (Hrushovski) in terms that particularly fit my own view of realism. For example, by an *Internal Field of Reference* (IFR), Harshaw understands an interrrelated and varied composite or network of elements—characters, events, situations, spaces, ideas, dialogues, etc.—that the language of the text institutes from the first sentence at the same time that it refers to it: "A work of literature can be defined as a verbal text which projects at least one Internal Field of Reference (IFR) to which meanings in the text are related" (Harshaw 1984, 235). The IFR is shaped according to various aspects of the physical, social, and human reality, with the decisive intervention of what Siegfrid J. Schmidt (1980, 1984) calls "ortho-world-model" (OWM), or socialized models of the world. Thus, through the reader's actualizations, one could translate the intensional and autonomous IFR in terms of the external or extensional field of reference (EFR) or reality ("the real world in time and space, history, a philosophy, ideologies, views of human nature, other texts" (Harshaw 1984, 243). It is, of course, the reality of the reader, who will decode the literary work in a certain way, emphasizing one or the other field of reference. Harshaw uses as an example Gibbon's *Decline and Fall of the Roman Empire*, which can be both a fascinating narrative and a historical document. In this sense, one can affirm that "'fiction' is not opposed to 'fact'" (Harshaw 1984, 237).

One can clearly apply Harshaw's theoretical framework to a concept of literary realism that is free of both the genetic and the formal fallacy. During the intentionally realistic reading of a given text, the internal field of reference is projected as being parallel to an external field of reference. So "parallel planes never meet" (Harshaw 1984, 248) except, I would add, in the reader's intentional consciousness. One can thus easily explain why fictional characters make real people cry, laugh, lose their sleep or peace of mind—a question that K. L. Walton's "How Remote Are Fictional Worlds from the Real World?" (1978, 12) presents as aporetic. Christopher Prendergast (1986, 61) points out, however, that the mimetic or realist text "knits the order of 'fiction' into the order of 'fact,' and thus ensures that process of recognition whereby the reader connects the world produced by the text with the world of which he himself has direct or indirect knowledge."

The Principle of Realist Cooperation

So we have come closer to an understanding of realism from the perspective of the reader (rather than that of the author or that of the isolated text), a perspective fully supported by a phenomenology that confers ontological plenitude on a literary work only when this work is actualized and by a pragmatics that considers meaning not merely in terms of assertions but, rather, in terms of a dialectic of assertion, reception, and referent. This is a realism in act, in which the recipient's activity is a decisive factor, being one of the most salient manifestations of the "principle of cooperation," first formulated by H. P. Grice (1975, 41–58), read in its unpublished version by Teun A. van Dijk (1976, 44), and later applied by J.-K. Adams (1985, 44) specifically to the field of literary fiction. The basic idea behind this principle is that of linguistic behavior as a type of intentional social interaction, directed by a cooperative will, which J. Lyons, following Grice, exemplifies by interpreting the phrase "John is a tiger" in a metaphorical key proper to it (Lyons 1981, 215). The fictional pact or the voluntary suspension of disbelief instituted by the literary *epoché* responds to this cooperative principle, and so does the projection of the EFR on the textual IFR, as well as, in phenomenological terms, the essentially schematic condition of the literary work of art, to which we shall turn shortly.

First, however, I would like to stress the fact that, because of the cooperative impulse, the reader tends to relate the intensional world of the text to his or her own world, i.e., to the purely extensional referent. Grice adds that all the agents of a standard linguistic communication expect a rational, serious, and cooperative type of behavior from one another; translated into the literary field, this would imply the reader's spontaneous and natural reception of a literary work as a serious assertion, so that this work, although fictitious, or even fantastic, would still be susceptible of a realist decoding. Such a decoding would involve the hermeneutic task of giving a realist meaning to the text, illuminating its immanent IFR from the standpoint of the EFR, according to the vision and interpretation of the multiple and varied reality of each individual reader (Cf. Taléns 1986, 15). Let this audacious conjecture (in Karl R. Popper's sense of the phrase) stand, until such time as new developments will rebutt, rectify, or ratify it.

Although Roman Ingarden does not figure in the theoretical horizon projected by Harshaw's study, one can nevertheless find in it at least two implicit references to Ingarden's phenomenological concept of the literary work of art. For example, when Harshaw shows the advantages of his theory of internal and external fields of reference over "possible worlds" semantics, he stresses above all that in his approach "a direct link is created between the projected (or 'intentional') 'world' and linguistic reference, hence between the ontology of literature and the analysis of language" (1984, 243), thus invoking the phenomenological concept of intentionality. Harshaw touches upon other aspects of the schematic and multilayered structure of the literary work of art as described by Ingarden's phenomenology and Wolfgang Iser's theory of the reading process (1976), when, referring to the manner in which the IFR and the EFR relate to each other, he says: "even if all the streets named in a novel are real streets, their selection creates an isolated cluster and there will be indoor settings unique in the IFR. Though modeled upon external examples, its field is unique and internally coherent" (1984, 249).

Realism and the Structure of the Literary Work

According to Roman Ingarden (1931, § 8), as we have seen, the structure of the literary work of art consists of several heterogeneous layers that differ from one another in their specific material and function—a difference lending them an essentially polyphonic, rather than a loose or disconnected, character. Two of these layers are of a purely verbal nature (Ingarden 1931, § 9–31): the layer of phonetic-linguistic formations and that of the semantic units. The first layer, apart from the aesthetic value it may acquire through a play on its rythmic qualities, which vary from one literary genre to another, basically serves as a support and external scaffold to the second one. This second layer makes it possible for a psychological subject to apprehend the work, starting from each semantic unit and performing an intentional act of sense-giving that involves the creation of a purely intentional objectivity: the represented world.

Ingarden (1931, § 31) adds, moreover, that the layer of the semantic units becomes completely "absorbed," as it were, because of its exclusive devotion to the task of constituting the next layers, so that it disappears within the whole work as something imperceptible in itself. In fact, both in standard language and in reading a literary work, we use the semantic content of words in order to arrive at the objective relation, or simply at the object these words may refer to. Ingarden believes this is the most compelling reason why a literary work can never be a completely a-rational product, as other types of art works, such as musical ones, can. The difference is that in literature, because its expressive medium is language, one must move beyond it, toward the other, non-linguistic layers of the work.

The third layer, which Ingarden (1931, § 32) calls the layer of "represented objectivities" (*Die Schicht der dargestellten Gegenständlichkeiten*), is precisely that of the intentional references projected by the prior layer of semantic units, mediating the reader's actualizations. Of course, these objectivities are not real, although they may seem so because the reader—who, according to Ingarden, remains fundamentally anchored in this layer—instills them with all the characteristics and properties of real objects; but this seemingly real quality can never be identified with that of the ontological order of existing entities. The city of "Munich" appearing in a literary text is not the objectively existing "Munich" that the reader may know from direct, personal experience (Ingarden 1931, § 34), but only "like" it. There is, in principle, a fundamental difference: the represented object—be it Munich or any other—is a schematic creation, with various gaps of indeterminacy (*Unbestimmtheitsstellen*). Thus, Ingarden makes a crucial theoretical assertion, indispensable for a phenomenological and pragmatic theory of realism: any literary work is essentially incomplete with respect to the objectivities presented in it, requiring an intensive and practically inexhaustible, cooperative complementation (here one should recall Grice's principle). During the process of reading, the recipient transcends the text, overcoming its representational deficiencies by eliminating a certain number of uncertainty gaps or lacunae, according to his or her competence, attitude, and interest. In some cases, the filling in of representational blanks is necessary for a succesful reading, but the text can also contain optional *Unbestimmtheitsstellen*.

Closely related to the schematic character of the literary work of art is Ingarden's last layer (1931, § 43–45): that of the aspects (*Ansichten*) under which the intentional objectivities referred to in the previous layer are represented. These aspects, which are also schematic, play a double role in the literary work: on the one hand, they influence the way in which the objectivities are presented and, on the other hand, they provide specific aesthetic qualities. In fact, for Ingarden (1931, § 63) the main difference between the literary work and its concretizations occurs in this layer. From the simple state of disponibility and schematism within the work itself, the aspects reach the concrete sphere through the recipient's actualizations, rising up to the living experience of perception (in the theater) or the imagination (in the other genres) and producing a vivid impression of realism; for, as Dominique Combe (1985, 44) argues, "en forçant un peu la thèse d'Ingarden," it is precisely "les éléments mimétiques du réel qui opèrent la fonction schématique: les aspects schématiques sont charactérisés par des 'qualités descriptives' analogues au réel."

Schematism and Actualization

In addition to this sort of transversal dissection of the work showing us its structure, Roman Ingarden also concentrates on its "longitudinal" or syntagmatic side, which is that of an actualization; because, as he points out at the end of his study (1931, § 68), "the work of art only constitutes an *aesthetic* object in a true sense *when it reaches its expression in a concretization*" ("Den *ästhetischen* Gegenstand in echtem Sinne bildet das literarische Kunstwerk *erst dann, wenn es in einer Konkretisation zur Ausprägung gelangt*"). From the perspective of realism, the most important effect of concretization is that it confers a real and explicit presence upon the represented objectivities that are merely outlined in the work, being subject to certain aspects (*Ansichten*) and thus buried in a state of potentiality.

In sum, since the literary work of art is a highly complex structure, its actualization implies multiple acts of consciousness. The most elementary one is the recipient's perception of the linguistic signs (sounds, words, formations of a superior order, and so forth), coupled with the apprehension of the significations carried by them. Finally, there are the acts of the imaginative intuition of the represented objectivities and situations that transform the text into a universe *of* and *for* the reader.

As Ingarden (1931, § 62) convincingly argues, through our acts of concretization we purge our consciousness of any perturbing influence, suspending all of our daily experiences and psychic states, as though we needed to blind and deafen ourselves to everything that comes from the real world. And Ingarden concludes with a very pertinent observation that brings us back to our argument regarding fields of reference and possible worlds: the literary work of art is "a true miracle" (*ein wahres Wunder*) because, even though it barely possesses an ontologically heteronomous existence, being completely dependent on us, its potential readers, and passively undergoing all the operations that we perform on it, it nevertheless produces important effects and modifications in our lives, liberating us from, and elevating us above, the banality of everydayness.

Here I have only summarized Ingarden's complex and systematic theory, which he frequently couches in a difficult, abstract language, but this summary is useful in revealing the phenomenological roots of the efficient instrument that Benjamin Harshaw provides for us in our search for a pragmatic revision of literary realism. In fact, even if we leave aside the two linguistic planes obvious in Harshaw's theory, I think there is a clear correspondence between his "Internal Field of Reference" (IFR) and Ingarden's layers of represented objectivities and the aspects under which they appear; in turn, the schematic state of these layers, requiring the reader's cooperative approach as well as his intentional projection on the text as a polyphonic whole, point unequivocally to Harshaw's complementary "External Field of Reference" (EFR).

The Act of Reading

Iser's theory in *Der Akt des Lesens* (1976), already presented in part in his contribution to a collective volume edited by Rainer Warning (1975; cf. also Iser 1975b), is also rooted in Ingarden's thought. Therefore, it can easily fit the present phenomenological and pragmatic approach to realism, an approach that J. D. Lyons and S. G. Nichols (1982, 3) wished to strengthen a few years ago ("we now stress the subjective and intellective role of the reader/viewer in mimetic theory") and Tzvetan Todorov (1975, 417) has also defended: "Ce qui existe, d'abord, c'est le texte, et rien que lui; ce n'est qu'en le soumettant à un type particulier de lecture que nous construisons, à partir de lui, un univers imaginaire."

For Iser, as for Todorov, the literary work provides the reader, through its language, with sufficient elements for "the building of a situation and so for the production of an imaginary context." Literary signs do not designate objects, but rather offer "instructions for the *production* of the signified," so that "the involvement of the reader is essential to the fulfillment of the text" (Iser 1976, 64–66). The text is like a living organism—"an array of sign impulses" (1976, 67)—that "instructs" and "programs" the reader, on whom it depends for its full existence through successive actualizations; a plenitude the text can reach, as Iser points out in a much cited passage (1976, 69), only by the convergence of a *repertoire* and a number of specific *strategies* with the "realization" proper.

It is not always easy to ascertain the exact range of Iser's formulations, perhaps because they suffer from a degree of *contaminatio* from phenomenological language, the main virtue of which is certainly not simplicity. In the passage just cited, however, the meaning of "realization" is evident: it denotes the reader's participation as actualizer of the text. What Iser calls "the process of reading" is "a *dynamic interaction* between text and reader," but a "successful communication must ultimately depend on the reader's creative activity" (1976, 107–112). Ideally, this creative activity consists in filling out Ingarden's *Unbestimmtheitsstellen*. In the work, "we have a sequence of schemata, built up by the repertoire and the strategies, which have the function of stimulating the reader himself into establishing the 'facts'" (1976, 141). We need to produce the context or referent projected by the textual scheme because "the meaning of the literary work remains related to what the printed text says, but it requires the creative imagination of the reader to put it all together" (1976, 142). And this creative imagination—a form of intentional consciousness—works above all with "the gaps in the text," or "the blanks which the reader is to fill in" (1976, 169). Iser defines a *Leerstelle* as "an empty space which both provokes and guides the ideational activity. In this respect, it is a basic element of the interaction between text and reader" (1976, 194–195).

What Iser means by "strategies," however, remains somewhat unclear to me. Upon a first reading, they seem to be the procedures that organize the internal world of the text, and my question here, as in other parts of Iser's argument, is whether these strategies belong to the author, who employs them in constructing his discourse and then leaves them as traces in the text, or to the reader, who uses them in order to actualize the work. The same question can be asked about Iser's repertoire, which I believe should ultimately be identified with Harshaw's interplay of the internal and the external fields of reference. In fact, Iser does invoke the "referential system of the repertoire," which results from that other dialectic between intrinsic and extrinsic textual elements. He argues that "the determinacy of the repertoire supplies a meeting point between text and reader" (1976, 69), adding that this repertoire consists of a selection of rules and references that cannot be arbitrary and must be related to reality.

But Iser's comment on the word "reality" is particularly interesting here: "The term reality is already suspect in this connection, for no literary text relates to contingent reality as such, but to models or concepts of reality, in which contingencies and complexities are reduced to a meaningful structure. We call these structures world-pictures or systems" (1976, 70). In other words, Iser's repertoire coincides with the third discourse that I have mentioned in regard to Aristotelian *mimesis*, the Marxist theory of reflection, and Peirce's interpretant. Let me emphasize, moreover, that it does not contradict but, rather, complements Harshaw's theory of reference fields.

The Realist Paradox

What one may label the "paradox of literary realism" arises precisely from the schematic condition of the literary work, which is a composite of both present or full elements and absent or empty ones. Together they constitute the paradox, just as they constitute the intentional universe that challenges us. The typographical blanks between chapters, or the immaculate reglets between lines of poetry, operate in this double direction, just as do the chapters and the lines themselves. Roman Ingarden has also studied this question in relation to Thomas Mann's story, "Tristan," in his second treatise on literary phenomenology (1968, § 27). If we apply Ingarden's argument to realism, the paradox resides in the fact that this literary phenomenon depends more on what the text lacks than on what it contains. As Héctor-Neri Castañeda (1979, 35) observes, "Real objects are complete . . . fictional objects, on the other hand, are incomplete." Or, if one prefers John Heintz's formulation (1979, 92), in contrast to reality, "fictional worlds are not only incomplete, they are sometimes inconsistent."

Because of this paradox, although a literary work of art may be a fictive, schematic discourse which constructs an autonomous world (IFR) as a text foreign to an outside context (EFR), one of its most remarkable and privative features is, in Barbara Hernstein Smith's words, "to invite and enable the reader to create a plausible context for it" (1971, 275). According to Hernstein Smith, reading consists of "this process of inference, conjecture, and indeed creation of contexts," just as a painter's conventional pattern of lines and colors depends on our habits of visual perception, or on our "reproductive competence" so to speak, to become a tridimensional scene, body, or object. So Milton does not produce Eve or the garden of Eden, but concise phrases "that lead the reader to create a woman and a place." Poetic language—and literary language in general—demands a constant intentional, imaginative, and hermeneutic cooperation on the reader's part in order to complete its meaning with "an appropriately rich, subtle, and coherent context of human feelings" (Hernstein

Smith 1971, 277). These feelings are derived from our own experiences of the world (which, of course, are not the same for every reader), so that, as Félix Martínez Bonati (1980, 30) points out, even though we may acknowledge that the characters and events represented are fictitious, once inside the literary work, "we view those persons and events as real ones."

In relation to realism, however, we need to determine the precise meaning of the term "referent." In previous chapters, in examining various notions of literary realism I have favored the conceptualizations of reality proposed by relativist or constructivist epistemologies. Instead of unreflectively postulating a consistent and unequivocal world accessible to the subject's direct perception, I have invoked the mediating presence of a third discourse which consists of the modalization, construction, or interpretation of the world, being already embedded in Aristotelian *mimesis*. I have also invoked, in this regard, Peirce's semiotic concept of interpretant (cf. Umberto Eco 1975, 133–140). Taléns and Company (1985, 218) also allude to this concept when they say that "the 'referent' is not the 'object itself' but, rather, our own way of acting upon objects, of manipulating and shaping them as an implicit correlative of language." Harshaw's EFR is equally an "interpretant," and so is Schmidt's OWM or, generally, Iser's "repertoire" (1976, 69), which Iser identifies with the Prague structuralists' "extratextual reality," including not only the empirical, social, and historical world, but also the artistic and literary universe of previous works of art.

Both Inge Crosmann (1983) and Mieke Bal (1984), moreover, coincide as to the relevance of the interpretant to the issue at hand. For Crossman, fictional works immerse their readers into a complex system of references and inferences: "Seen this way the literary referent is a floating, conceptual construct that gradually emerges during the reading process through textual guidance and the reader's active collaboration. It is an 'interpretant' and not a reference to a thing, person, or prior state of affairs" (1983, 96). Indeed, it is always something *a posteriori*, rather than *a priori* (as genetic realism has claimed). Likewise, Mieke Bal believes that "the construction of reality in fiction is in the first place a problem of subject(act)ivity" (1984, 338); but, in view of the most recent interpretations of Aristotelian *mimesis*, such as that of Roselyne Dupont-Roc and Jean Lallot (Aristotle 1980), she also believes that "reading fiction is the attribution of an interpretant to a mimetic sign" (Bal 1984, 371).

In any case, from the perspective of the present study, literary realism is mainly a pragmatic phenomenon resulting from the individual reader's projection of a vision of the external world upon an intensional world suggested by the text. This is why Paul Ricoeur's interpretation of *mimesis* (1981) stresses the kinship of this term with *poiesis* and *praxis* (reinforced by their common suffix, *-is*), giving the world a sense of productive, rather than duplicative, reference (cf. Prendergast 1986, 234–238). The rightful defense of the autonomy of the literary intensional universe does not require denying that literature speaks of reality to its addressees, or, put in a different way, that readers make literature refer to their reality. Neither does such a view neglect the author's perspective, which would engender the genetic fallacy only if it became the *prima ratio* of realism.

It is a fact, moreover, that the recipient's intentionality (as well as his EFR) can coincide with that of the creator of the text and its corresponding IFR. Susana Reisz de Rivarola (1979, 144) points out, however, that this "is only guaranteed when the addressee—either because he is the creator's contemporary and a member of the same cultural community, or because an effort has been made to shorten the hermeneutic distance between them—is in a position to operate with a notion of reality similar to that of the creator; when he has the literary competence of recognizing fiction as such, as well as the particular poetics upon which that notion rests; and, consequently, when he can co-intentionally perform the creator's intentional modifications exactly in the terms stipulated by the latter."

This kind of co-intentionality, whereas perfectly possible, is nevertheless much less common in realistically actualized texts than the reader's exclusive intentionality, because, as I have already suggested, the author's intentionality is not a decisive factor in itself. And, like almost everything else in literary theory, my suggestion is already embedded in Aristotle's *Poetics* (1448b, 12–19), when he praises recognition as one of the pleasures produced by imitation: "For, in effect, not only the philosophers rejoice, but men in general observing the images, because as it happens, watching them, they learn and deduce which is which, for example that this is that, for if one has not seen the portrayed before, it will not produce pleasure as imitation, but because of the execution, or the color, or some other reason."

4

INTENTIONAL REALISM

It is perhaps appropriate to recall, at this point, the general principle that ought to guide us in considering not only literary realism but also literary studies as a whole, namely the necessary interdependence between literary theory and the applied fields of literary history and criticism. Unless they are firmly rooted in general or abstract principles, literary history and criticism can easily fall into casuistics, impressionism, or erudition for its own sake; in turn, literary theory must never lose sight of the reality of texts, which determines its usefulness and without which it runs the risk of arbitrariness and logomachy. Therefore, we need constantly to move back and forth between theoretical abstraction and the empirical corroboration of concrete literary phenomena.

Two Examples: Pereda and Blasco Ibáñez

The phenomenological and pragmatic theory of realism that I have envisaged here requires particularly careful treatment. My point of departure was the dissatisfaction that many of us have experienced, as readers and literary scholars, with the postulates of the genetic and formal types of realism, which I have attempted to transcend by viewing this fundamental literary phenomenon as a product of the reader's active cooperation. I still need to determine if this cooperation does in fact occur in the theoretical terms that I have proposed—a task that I shall take up later on in this book. For the moment, let me turn to textual cases that show the realism-producing mechanism at work, projecting the reader's external field of reference or interpretant upon the created, autonomous universe of the literary work.

The first example concerns a sort of foreword which José María de Pereda included in the first edition (1885) of his novel *Sotileza* (Fishing Cord) and in which he did not address all of his readers, but only "my contemporaries from Santander who may still be alive." I am not unaware that this foreword is fraught with the kind of suspicions and prejudices against criticism that Pereda voiced only too often, but this fact—which is largely anecdotal anyway—does not prevent it from being a very useful case for my pragmatic theory of realism. Pereda acknowledges his mimetic intention to "present cases and things of human life in imaginative works," an intention that in this specific instance acquires certain "archeological" overtones, as it were. For *Sotileza* "is nothing but an excuse to resurrect individuals, things, and places that hardly exist anymore, and to reconstruct a town which, during its patriarchal rest, has become buried, almost overnight, under a huge pile of foreign ideas and customs that the torrent of a new and strange civilization has dragged up to it." (Ed. E. Miralles. Madrid: Alhambra, 1977, 60).

Pereda implicitly acknowledges that he has shaped the internal universe of *Sotileza* according to a vision of the world and society—or, as Siegfried Schmidt would say, a certain "ortho-world-model"—which is threatened with extinction. Indeed, the traditional, patriarchal society that he nostalgically contemplates has largely given way to another social system—the bourgeois, industrial one—all over Europe, although in Spain in a less resolute manner than elsewhere. So Pereda adds that only his contemporary fellow countrymen can understand his purpose and can co-intentionally recreate the world presented in his novel together with the generations that shaped it: "To whom but to all of you who knew them alive should I grant the competence necessary to ascertain whether or not their language was truly the one spoken within these pages; whether or not their customs, laws, vices and virtues, souls and bodies were those presented here?" (1977, 61). In no way can we expect the same understanding from other readers, especially the younger ones or those outside the Cantabrian region, whom Pereda rather sarcastically calls "distinguished and sophisticated," attributing to them the new worldview. One may note, however, that precisely such readers will project on *Sotileza* an interpretant that goes against the author's will but that, despite that will (and herein lies the paradox), gives the novel its full meaning.

Pereda, although sensitive to criticism and not adverse to speculations about the intricacies of literary creation, was obviously no theorist, which does not prevent the text under consideration from having great theoretical value. It is remarkable, for instance, that Pereda should use the word *competence* in terms that are perfectly comparable to the theoretical jargon borrowed from linguistics, *à la page* during the nineteen sixties and seventies. Pereda even asks for the addressee's active cooperation in the reading process, required by the schematism of the work: "And who but all of you can subtitute faithful memory for what cannot be represented with the pen: the accent of halting speech; the frowning expression without malevolence; the salty ambiance of the person, voice, gestures and untidy clothing? And should it happen, taking into consideration both what I cannot represent here, because it surpasses human powers, and what I can, that the figures be complete and alive, who but all of you would be able to know it?" (1977, 61). Pereda's rhetorical question brings us back to our main point: he offers us an intuitive testimony, *avant la lettre*, of the pragmatic operation of literary realism that consists in the creation, starting from an author's experiences, of an intensional world or internal field of reference that will complete its meaning only when the extensional interpretant—rather than referent—of a reader who is as close as possible to the novelist himself is intentionally projected upon it.

Pereda, moreover, concludes his foreword with a predictable declaration: "So may God forgive me for having thought of no other readers but you when I wrote this book. And once this said, let it be also said that I subject it solely to your judgement and expect solely your verdict" (1977, 59). Of course, this declaration hides a utopia. Every Santanderian born, like Pereda, in 1833 and sharing the same development, social class, culture, and ideological attitude, would still project on the IFR of *Sotileza* a different EFR. I have already shown that it cannot be otherwise, in my critique of

Schleiermacher's "hermeneutics of reconstruction" within a context that was different, yet not unrelated to the present one. Let us also recall Hegel's expressive metaphor in *Phänomenologie des Geistes* (1807, 435–436): literary works of art are like "fine fruits fallen from a tree," for, with the passing of time, they preserve only a veiled and blurry memory of the reality from which they came. And Gadamer's phenomenologically inspired statement (1965, 471) brings us even closer to pragmatics: "Comprehensive reading does not mean repeating something past, but participating in a present meaning."

One may also note that the main problem with Pereda's type of realism in *Sotileza* comes from one of the essential characteristics of literary language, namely that it is "out of context." The chronological gap between the existential situation of the transmitter and that of the recipient is present even among contemporaries, and the problem—or "noise," in terms of information theory—is aggravated by the absence of contact between them and by the impossibility of the metalinguistic function suggested by Pereda. Everything must then be left to the discretion of the reader's hermeneutic function, which is individually, spatially, and chronologically independent and variable.

Along the same lines, one can consider the unusual case of Vicente Blasco Ibáñez's novel, *La voluntad de vivir* (The Will to Live), recently analyzed by Ricardo Senabre (1987, 30–32). Although its imminent publication was announced in 1907, the novel was not released in its integral form until sixty years later, in the fourth volume of Blasco Ibáñez's complete works (there is also an earlier edition—Madrid: Planeta, 1953—but it is badly mutilated by censorship). Libertad Blasco Ibáñez, in a brief preface to the complete first edition, offers the following explanation for this unusual editorial delay: "Before releasing his novels, Blasco Ibáñez had the habit of offering his friends the gift of a reading, in order to get their opinions prior to those of the critics and the public. This time they all agreed: Morote, Benlliure, Sorolla, Canalejas, Amalio Gimeno, and other close friends saw in the protagonist, the wise doctor 'Enrique Valdivia,' the portrait of a great Spanish physician, a luminary of world medicine, whom Blasco Ibáñez loved and admired as a close friend despite the age difference between them: don Luis Simarro Lacabra." Blasco Ibáñez repeatedly complained that he had never had the intention of portraying his eminent friend; the protagonist was the sole product of his imagination, mere fiction. But his wife sided with his friends and told him that "Dr. Simarro might get offended. . . . The author could not afford . . . a scandal and *understood that people would see only what they wanted to see.* He withdrew the novel and had the whole edition burnt" (Libertad Blasco Ibáñez, in Blasco Ibáñez, *Obras completas.* Madrid: Aguilar, 1977, pp. 694–695. My emphasis).

Owing to this valuable first-hand testimony, it is easy to see that the IFR of *La voluntad de vivir* includes an autonomous character, Dr. Enrique Valdivia, created by the author's imagination, but that, even before the publication of the book, several readers—all friends of the novelist—projected on the text an EFR in which this character became the unmistakable likeness of a real individual, Dr. Luis Simarro. Translated into our terms, this means that the readers' intentional projection, not co-intentional with the novelist's, tended to transform *La voluntad de vivir* into a veritable *roman à clef*, a tendency that had been encouraged, since the beginning of the century, by Blasco Ibáñez's own urban novels, located in Jerez, Toledo, and Madrid.

This genre of "novels with a code" is highly useful in analyzing the processes of intentional realism. Thus, María del Carmen Bobes Naves (1985b, 13) explains the scandal around the publication of Leopoldo Alas's *La Regenta* as a consequence of a certain reading attitude on the part of Alas's contemporaries, "which prevented the novel from being seen as a work of art, for the reading was limited to that of a testimonial text, the univocal character of which the readers wanted at any cost." An earlier example of the same phenomenon is invoked by Gustavo Adolfo Bécquer, a poet who was conscious of the complex processes of literary creation. In his article "Las dos olas" (The Two Waves), initially published in *La Ilustración de Madrid* and later included in his *Obras completas* (Madrid: Aguilar, 1969; 13th ed., pp. 684–690), Bécquer discusses Casado de Alisal's portrait of a girl, reproduced in *La Ilustracion*, disagreeing with the artist. Whereas the latter considers it to be an occasional piece, made on request on the Biarritz beach, Bécquer discerns in it a totally different, much more transcendent meaning—the mysterious representation of femininity. The poet will not give up his reading even when learning of the portrait's origin and the artist's intention: "You speak of it as being similar; I don't know whether it is like the original, but it is pretty and that is enough; it certainly resembles something, but not this or that person about whom I, an indifferent beholder, do not care; rather, *it resembles the ideal of beauty, of which we all have the pattern in our soul. . . . When I admire the portrait of a beautiful woman by Van Dyck, I never ask: 'Does it look like the original?' What do I care? It looks like those women whom I have not seen, but whom I have dreamt about, and who already recall a beloved image"* (my emphasis).

In *The Mirror and the Lamp*, M. H. Abrams (1953, 20) lists a simple (but erroneous) diagram representing the inter-relations of reality, the work of art, its author, and its audience:

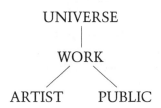

The major problem with this diagram is that it posits an exclusive relationship between the work and the universe, linking this universe (without specifying whether it is a real or a "possible" world) with the artist and his addressees solely through the work. Kathryn Hume (1984, 9) also points out Abrams's inconsistencies, arguing for the existence of two worlds: that of the author ("world 1") and that of the reader ("world 2"). These worlds "differ even if the artist and reader are contemporaries; world 2 indeed differs for each member of the audience. If artist and audience are separated by time, language, religion, culture, or class, the amount of shared reality may be small. The nature of what each considers significant reality will overlap even less. The Universe or world within the work differs yet again."

In turn, Hume (1984, 10) proposes her own diagram, which is much more complex and more accurate than Abrams's and which, for me, has the additional interest of representing the reciprocal influence between "world 1" and the author, as well as that of "world 2" on the reader (see Figure 4.1). I certainly acknowledge the usefulness of Hume's diagram, but I believe it would not be entirely inappropriate to suggest my own, because although we share a similar concept of realism, I use a different critical metalanguage, including phenomenology, pragmatics, and semantic logic (see Figure 4.2).

If we examine the three columns of my diagram, the first column would fall within the sphere of what I have called "genetic realism" ("correspondence realism") and the second one, within the sphere of formal or immanent realism. The third type of realism, defined from the standpoint of phenomenology and pragmatics, is not reflected in the third printed column, but throughout the diagram, which summarizes my argument so far. This third type I have called "intentional realism."

The Epistemology of the Literary Work

We can now go back, for a moment, to the epistemology of the verbal work of art and the different modalities of its apprehension, as developed by Roman Ingarden in his second treatise (1968). This is the phenomenological aspect most clearly related to pragmatics and is crucial for our theory of realism in act, or intentional realism, in which the final responsibility and decision rest with the reader, regardless of the author's intention, for, as Roland Barthes puts it, the literary work "est toujours en situation prophétique." María del Carmen Bobes Naves (1985, 219) shares this viewpoint in her study of *La Regenta*: "It is possible that from the perspective of the reader's competence, the meaning of a work will not coincide with the one intended by the author, because once a narrative becomes independent as a cultural, objective product, it

FIGURE 4.1

Reciprocal Influence Between World 1 and World 2

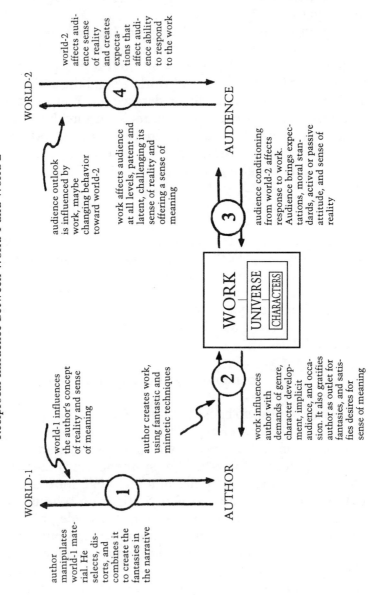

FIGURE 4.2

Intentional Realism

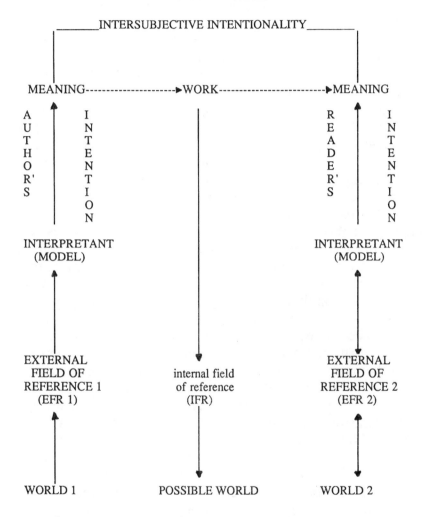

can relate to extratextual realities that change according to
the period, the culture, or the reader." Let us also recall that
when the contract of co-intentionality is frequently broken,
the recipient's intention will prevail. Thus, the text's open-
ness to the projection of successive contexts on the part of its
readers leads most often to intentional realism, in my sense of
the term.

Ingarden's phenomenological epistemology makes a crucial distinction (1968, § 26) between the work as an artistic object—or a text in a potential state—and the work as an aesthetic object, i.e., as completely actualized through the cooperation of the reader who resolves its indeterminacies and corrects its schematism. For Ingarden, therefore, the artistic values belong to the "inert" text, whereas the aesthetic values are revealed through an appropriate actualization of the work. Although the text "instructs" its addressee to that purpose, the form of this instruction is seldom precise or free of ambiguities (1968, 252), so that there will never be two identical actualizations of the same work—even if they belong to the same reader—nor will any actualization as an "aesthetic object" ever coincide exactly with the "artistic object" that inspires it.

As I have already pointed out, in the process of the apprehension of the literary work of art (a process that varies considerably according to the literary genre), the layer of phonetic formations usually remains embedded in the semantic layer, which the reader should understand without excessive difficulty if his linguistic competence is adequate. In the semantic layer, however, there originates the difficult task of intentionally projecting the objectivities and aspects that constitute the world of the literary work and center the readers' attention. Its schematic character accounts for the differences in actualization that separate one reading from another, something that Lázaro de Tormes had already been aware of when deciding to tell us his life story, "for it could be that some readers will find in it something to please them, and others, who merely dip in it, may find it delightful." (But we shall return to Lázaro shortly.) The main difference between a literary work of art and its concretizations, moreover, is that in the latter its potential elements are actualized and its gaps of indeterminacy filled (R. Ingarden 1968, 241). And finally, as we have seen, Ingarden (1968, § 25) distinguishes four possible forms of contact with, or cognition of, the literary work: 1) the an-aesthetic or extra-aesthetic experience of a "literary consumer"; 2) the aesthetic experience of a common reader; 3) the pre-aesthetic cognition of the work through literary reasearch; 4) the cognition of an aesthetic concretization in its full plenitude.

Intentional Realism as Natural Response

Ingarden (1968, 282) returns to this classification (which, simple as it may seem, is not devoid of difficulties) in a chapter-long paragraph (§ 27) in which he refers to realism several times in relation to Thomas Mann's *Buddenbrooks*. Ingarden essentially says that most readers will focus on the represented objectivities, at the expense of the other layers that are superficially experienced, whereas "a philologically and linguistically oriented reader hardly notices the portrayed objectivities and the aspects in which they appear. For him, the peculiarities of the language will move into the foreground."

Ingarden's observation is particularly useful for my pragmatic thesis, leading me to differ from Susana Reisz de Rivarola's otherwise illuminating causal analysis of fictionality. What Reisz de Rivarola has to say in this respect deserves to be quoted at length: "The reception of literary fictions is a highly complex phenomenon comprising a wide variety of reactions to the modifications proposed by the text. Complete lack of competence on the reader's part would result in a total failure of communication, in not recognizing fiction for what it is. A rather low level of competence would imply a recipient who would be capable of recognizing the fictional character of the text, but not the particular poetics that supports it, and would limit himself to identifying with the characters and participating affectively in their lives with the obscure awareness that 'this is not really happening' but it could happen. By contrast, a considerably higher degree of competence would imply a recipient who can clearly perceive the text in its textuality and not miss it among so many factors that trigger the illusion, and who can understand it in terms of the adaptation or rejection of certain literary-fictional conventions that occupy a precise place within the historical series" (1979, 168).

Here, of course, we are not concerned with fictionality as a specific topic, constrained by the parameters of semantic logic, but with a much broader issue that subsumes it: literary realism. So, unlike Reisz de Rivarola, we can make the conjecture (in the Popperian sense of the word) that the intentionally realistic decodification of a text is not only the most spontaneous, natural, and common one, but it also indicates a higher "aesthetic" competence (in Ingarden's sense) than formalist scepticism, which is more proper to what Ingarden understands by philological and linguistic competence, i.e., a critical, theoretical, or metaliterary one. Indeed, a "derealizing" mode of reading may be most common among a group of readers with the highest analytic capacity, who somehow reject the pact of the fictional *epoché*, appreciating the text solely for its building components. But other no less judicious and competent readers, who fully acknowledge the literary principle of formalist estrangement, may nevertheless allow themselves to be seduced by what the early Russian formalists never denied: the work as an epiphany of reality. Only a suspicious reader, wary of the intentional and affective fallacies and mindful solely of artistic artifice, would perform a deliberately anti-realist actualization of the literary work of art, or a "metareading." By contrast, the other reader, who has a no less rigorous and exhaustive knowlege of literary principles, would be willing to apprehend the work not only as an "artistic object" but also as an "aesthetic object" and, conforming to the *epoché* or voluntary suspension of disbelief, would accept a pact or convention that allows him to project his own empirical experience of reality on the fictional world, thus producing intentional realism.

From this perspective, any text, including the allegorical, symbolic, surrealist, or fantastic kinds, can be intended realistically because, behind the complex system of signs that the text is, there is always an actualizable and intentionable reference either to a reality of appearances or to a profound and essential one. Harry Levin (1972, 251), for example, considers that Kafka meets the requirements of realism in the highest sense of the word because he reveals the abysmal depths of the soul, which was a quality that Dostoyevsky also claimed for himself. And in the Spanish-speaking world, Antonio Risco (1987, 12 ff.) reaches similar conclusions in his study about Spanish fantastic literature, which, according to him, does not have a specific poetics, but turns out to be, just like so-called "realist literature," the product of a certain "mode of reading" (more or less induced by the text, however).

In the case of the "normal" reader, the process of realist intentional actualization is spontaneous. The very power of the written, and then printed, word suggests a form of veracity that stimulates realist intentionality, as Levin (1972, 248–251) also points out. Furthermore, Siegfried J. Schmidt (1976, 170–173) notes that "for a normal reader the story of an Earl of X in a newspaper is in no other way fictive than the story of Madame Bovary," because the way of constructing the fictional world that the literary work proposes requires "a permanent comparison of the modal status of the text world with EW ('our normal world system of experience,' p. 165)."

Schmidt makes another important statement to which I shall have occasion to return: "I cannot prove this hypothesis empirically; I can only refer to personal introspection and opinions of some people regarding their reading practice; yet I suppose that the normal reader continously (and mostly implicitly) compares W1 ['world or world system constituted by literary texts,' p. 16] to EW." Almost two centuries before Schmidt, Clara Reeve (1785), in her often quoted, but seldom read, *The Progress of Romance Through Times, Countries, and Manners; with Remarks on the Good and Bad Effects of it, on Them Respectively; in a Course of Evening Conversations*—an important work on the theory of the novel—maintained the same thesis that Schmidt develops from the perspective of what we now call "literary reception theory." Reeve is convinced that in modern romances "truth and fiction were so blended together that a common reader could not distinguish them" (1785, 65), because "the effects of romance, and true history are not very different. When the imagination is raised, men do not stand to enquire whether the motive be true or false" (1785, 102). Hence the need for the present-day warning, included in so many novels and feature films, that any similarity between fiction and fact should be viewed as merely coincidental.

Two More Examples:
Lazarillo de Tormes and *Don Quijote*

Of course, the kind of realism produced by the reader's intentional experience differs from the naive, or even pathological, realism produced by the reader's identification with the world supposedly lying behind the text—an identification that is amply documented in literary history, particularly in the wake of the popular success of chivalric romances. Thus, Alonso de Fuentes mentions an obsessed reader who knew the whole of *Palmerín de Oliva* by heart; Francisco de Portugal tells us how all the women in a gentleman's household welcomed him one day in grief over Amadís's death; and the Count of Guimerán recounts his meeting with a student who tried to defend, sword in hand, a paladin ambushed by a group of villains in the novel he was reading. In turn, Melchor Cano mentions a priest who believed everything he read in his books of chivalry, reasoning that if it were not true, the authorities would not allow it to be published—an argument that Juan Palomeque also offers to the Priest in *Don Quijote* (I, 32):

> A fine thing, your Grace's trying to make me believe that all these good books say is nothing but lies and foolishness, when they are printed with the license of the royal council! Do you mean to tell me they are the kind of folk who would consent to the printing of a lot of stories that are not true, with all those battles and enchantments and other things that are enough to drive a person crazy?

Later on, Don Quijote himself repeats the same argument in a conversation with the Canon of Toledo (I, 50):

> "That," replied Don Quixote, "is a fine thing to say! Do you mean to tell me that those books that have been printed with a royal license and with the approval of the ones to whom they have been submitted and which are read with general enjoyment and praised by young and old alike, by rich and poor, the learned and the ignorant, the gentry and the plain people—in brief, by all sorts of persons of every condition and walk in life—do you mean to tell me that they are but lies? Do they not have every appearance of being true? Do they not tell us who the father, mother, relatives of these knights were, the name

of the country from which they came, their age, the feats that they performed, point by point and day by day, and the places where all these events occurred?"

In relation to *Don Quijote*, which Francisco Abad Nebot (1980, 121 ff.) sees as belonging to a "realism of complexity," Nelson Goodman observes: "Taken literally, *Don Quixote* describes no one—there never was or will be the Man of La Mancha— but taken metaphorically, Don Quixote describes many of us who battle windmills (or windbags). A fantastic allegory, though an unrealistic fictive-person-story when read literally, may be a realistic real-person-story when taken metaphorically" (1983, 271–272). So Goodman equally emphasizes the reader's intentionality. When this intentionality favors realism, the text suggests the reality of what it presents, creating it as such, whereas the reader accepts it, providing his own referent. Siegfried J. Schmidt (1978) makes the same point, paraphrasing Götz Wienold: the reference issue does not primarily concern the combination of text and reality but, rather, the way in which readers use texts in order to make statements about their own reality. This is also an exact description of what I mean by "intentional realism."

But the best case in point is undoubtedly the first modern short novel, *La vida de Lazarillo de Tormes y de sus fortunas y adversidades* (The Life of Lazarillo de Tormes, and of His Fortunes and Adversities), on which Francisco Rico's most recent scholarship (1988) casts a new light. According to Rico, the first readers of this anonymous work (which started circulating in 1552 or 1553), being accustomed to books of chivalry and other stylized fantasies such as pastoral and sentimental romances, received *Lazarillo* as a true story, because within their horizon of literary expectations this kind of work was highly unusual and could only be accorded the status of truth. The masterful writer who produced it took advantage of the novelty of his story as a fictional work, presenting it "as if it were the authentic work of an authentic Lázaro de Tormes. Not just a verisimilar story, I insist, but a true one. Not realist, but real" (Rico 1988, 154).

According to Rico, the artist shows an extraordinary compositional ability, initially based on the fact, already implied by Américo Castro in his analysis of *Lazarillo*, that anonymity is solidary with autobiography. In order to preserve the full veracious force that an epistolary speech act possesses, the author hides himself, leaving behind him the protagonist of the story as the only subject of discourse. He further takes advantage of the general European passion, around 1500, of writing "messenger epistles." As Rico (1988, 155) notes, "letters were in themselves a form of expression reserved for the narration of real facts, and the disguise of a letter guaranteed *Lazarillo* an initial presumption of veracity."

But I must take exception with Rico's argument that the anonymous author of *Lazarillo de Tormes* deliberately seeks to deceive his readers. Quite the contrary, he gives his readers precisely what they want, because the intentional realist reading is a natural response, rather than a guided one, or even one stipulated in an implicit novelistic pact. There is no deceit when the victim is eager to be deceived, and in any case, the reader can devise a completely realistic interpretation of the text, for which *Lazarillo* provides numberless opportunities, especially if we take into account the natural context at the time of its publication.

Let us add the veracity effect of the printed word—and Rico does not fail to mention it—an effect that must have been particularly powerful in those days, when Gutenberg's invention had barely entered its second century of existence, and that lingers on even today, when our newspapers occasionally seem more to *create* than transcribe reality. So Rico (1988, 159) is certainly right when he argues that at the beginning of modernity, "the illusion of being confronted with a true reality, without mediations of any kind, never—never—had occured in the categorical terms of *Lazarillo*"; and that "theoretically, *Lazarillo de Tormes* does not *narrate* a real story: it *is* a real story, the real linguistic act of a real individual—who at times tells the truth and at times lies."

A similar phenomenon occurred in 1669—proving intentional realism to be a literary constant—when an ambitious editor, encouraged by the recent commercial success of François de Grenaille's book, *Nouveau recueil de lettres de dames tant anciennes que modernes* (1642), took out, from

Gabriel de Lavergne, Seigneur de Guilleragues's projected complete works, the volume of *Lettres d'amour d'une religieuse escrites au chevalier C. officier françois en Portugal* and published it anonymously. Thereby, the editor stimulated—no less than *Lazarillo de Tormes* and precisely because of its similar autobiographic and anonymous effects—a pragmatic, intentionally realist reading of these letters. What was originally a mere editorial trick by someone who perfectly understood the mechanism of realist intentionality (considering it as spontaneous and natural as I do) soon became not only a great commercial success, but also solid *reality*: the addressee of the letters was "identified" as Nöel de Chamilly, a French gentleman stationed in Portugal beginning in 1667, during the French expedition against Spain, an identification that Chamilly himself never denied. Moreover, in the nineteenth century the anonymous author's "true" identity was discovered: Mariana de Alcoforado, who died in the convent of the Conception of Beja around 1723. And so the famous *Lettres de la religieuse portugaise* were born, whose textual genesis and evolution confirm our theory of intentional realism.

The Referential Illusion

There are numerous other literary instances of intentional realism. Thus, Balzac, in the foreword to *Le père Goriot* (Paris: Livre de Poche, 1983, 6) addresses his readers in the following terms: "Vous qui tenez ce livre d'une main blanche, vous qui vous enfoncez un moelleux fauteuil en vous disant: Peut-être ceci va-t-il m'amuser. . . . Ah! sachez-le: ce drame n'est ni une fiction, ni un roman. All is true, il est si véritable, que chacun peut en reconnaître les éléments chez soi, dans son coeur peut-être."

In turn, the narrator of Tolstoy's *Anna Karenina* says that the essential element in reading a novel is to become interested in real feelings or emotions, starting from alien imaginary lives—a statement E. Hennequin, a French critic and Tolstoy's contemporary, paraphrases in 1888: "Le roman sera goûté, non à cause de la verité objective qu'il exprime, mais en raison du nombre de gens dont il réalisera la verité subjective,

dont il rend les idées, dont il ne contredit pas l'imagination."
Charles Grivel (1973, 251), from whom I have borrowed the
preceding quotation, also provides the example of Flaubert
praising Walter Scott because his readers, "sans connaître les
modèles, ils trouvaient ces peintures ressemblantes, et l'illusion était complète."

As I have already suggested, the *illusion référentielle*,
which the critics mistakenly locate in the text and which
should, according to Michael Riffaterre (Barthes et al. 1982,
93), be located in the reader "dans l'oeil de qui regarde—quand
elle n'est pas la rationalisation [here I would use the word
"intentionality" instead] du texte opérée par le lecteur"—is
inherent in every communicative event, being produced by
the perlocutionary, rather than the illocutionary, force of the
assertion. In this regard, the reaction of a contributor to *Le
radical* who witnessed the Lumière brothers' first film projection in public, in December 1895, seems very curious. To
him, their invention, consisting in a "reproduction, by means
of projection, of scenes lived and photographed through series
of instantaneous proofs," had appeared as highly exceptional,
because it allowed a return to seeing the models "in their natural size, with colors [sic], perspective, distant skies, houses,
streets, with all the illusion of real life" (cf. Juan Miguel
Company-Ramón 1986, 53–55).

Susan Fromberg Schaeffer (1980, 729) has also provided a
few examples of referential illusion that remind us of the passages from *Don Quijote* cited above. She confesses that her novel
Anya, which deals with the disasters of World War II, created
among her worldwide readers such an "illusion of absolute
authenticity" that she received letters in Polish from survivors of
that war asking her for information about individuals; a telephone call from an Australian lady who was convinced that the
novelist was her sister, lost during the war; and it even took her
publishers some time to accept the fact that she was not a
European in her fifties, but only a thirty-five year old American.

Furthermore, Thomas G. Pavel (1983, 84) demonstrates
the relative character of fictionality, definable only in pragmatic terms, by analyzing the first paragraph of Robert Musil's
Der Mann ohne Eigenschaften, which contains a technical

meteorological description of a beautiful summer day in August 1913. One can also mention Sigfried Schmidt who, in his article on the pragmatic interpretation of fictionality (1976, 177), records the most recent avant-garde efforts to integrate art into life, and life into art (i.e., happenings, art and language, etc.) until the border established by the principle of fictionality vanishes entirely; he then comments: "The future will show whether they can succeed." In the first volume of his *Grundriss der empirischen Literarturwissenschaft* (1980c, 72, n. 9), Schmidt casually mentions two specifically literary movements that can also illustrate our theory of intentional realism: the "non fiction novel" of Truman Capote and Norman Mailer and the "new journalism" of Tom Wolfe, Gay Talese, and Hunter Thomson, among others (the obvious connection between the two has been studied, for example, by John Hollowell—1977—although in a descriptive rather than a theoretical fashion). Finally, one can mention here such a latter-day tendency as "dirty realism," which equally blurs the line between fiction and reality.

Of course, such tendencies were not born in the sixties, having immediate precursors in George Orwell's *Homage to Catalonia* or Ernest Hemingway's *Green Hills of Africa* (in the foreword of which we read: "The writer has attempted to write an absolutely true book, to see whether the shape of a country and the pattern of a month's action can, if truly presented, compete with a work of imagination"). But there have been other, much earlier works, such as Daniel Defoe's, which their contemporaries viewed as authentic historical documents: *Journal of the Plague Year, Memoir of Cavaliers*, and *Robinson Crusoe*. In the Spanish world, one can cite the classic case of José María de Pereda's *Pachín González*; in a letter-preface of 1905 Pereda says that his novel's success was due to "the dreadful drama that it narrates, which, unfortunately, is historically accurate down to the smallest details," as well as to the fact that the reading public "is never tired of deep impressions and powerful emotions, such as those produced by the horrid catastrophe on that indescribable day, recorded forever in our memory," i.e., November 3, 1893, when the steamboat "Machichaco" blew up in the bay of Santander.

Epoché and Epiphany

From our point of view, the relativization of the limits between what is real and what is not is a most significant phenomenon. We have seen that readers treat this relativization as natural and that it has lately also become natural for the creative process, in the "non fiction novel," the "new journalism," or the "narrative-document." Hence the heated controversy around Truman Capote's *In Cold Blood* (1965), which faithfully narrates all the details surrounding the murder of the Clutter family in Holcomb, Kansas, on November 15, 1959. E. L. Doctorow also shows himself aware of this relativization in his acceptance speech for the Best 1975 Novel Award of the National Book Critics Circle, when he declares: "There is no more fiction or non fiction. Only narrative." (cf. Hollowell 1977, 3). Clas Zilliacus (1979) has called the same phenomenon "radical naturalism," citing, among other examples, the anthropologist Oscar Lewis's series about a Mexican family which began in 1961 with *The Children of Sanchez* and contained tape-recorded transcriptions of individual narrations by each of the family members. René Wellek (1982, 30) refers, in turn, to this curious and important development in one of his latest works on realism, which I have mentioned as an example of the anti-immanentist reaction present in current theoretical approaches to literature.

Realism in effect means conferring a realist meaning on a text from the referential horizon provided by each reader's experience of the world. Understanding, as Gadamer (1965, 414) points out, is a form of effect, and its scheme primarily includes a phase that is very important not only for legal and theological hermeneutics, but also for intentional realism, namely what was traditionally known as *subtilitas applicandi*, culminating with *subtilitas intelligendi* and *subtilitas explicandi* as interpretive phases proper. For Gadamer, as we have seen, the cognitive element of literary reading (i.e., of works of fiction) is crucial and not limited to recognition: "The joy of recognition is rather that more becomes known than is already known" (1965, 102).

Intentional realism as a result of the natural or—in Ingarden's terms—aesthetic actualizations of literature can be identified with what Karlheinz Stierle (1979, 301) rather pejoratively calls "quasi-pragmatic reception," half way between literary reception (as described by semioticians such as Götz Wienold) and pragmatic reception proper (which regards textual content as an instruction applicable to the external world). In his lesser-known commentaries on Aristotle's *Poetics*, Roman Ingarden (1961–62, 282–283) disagrees with those who understand *mimesis* as a mere copy, and not as a production of a "quasi-real" world, with an "objective consequence" (*gegenständliche Konsequenz*) for its recipients.

C. S. Lewis (1961, 23) also states that reaching beyond words for something non-verbal and non-literary does not seem to him a bad form of reading, as long as it does not lead to rejecting everything that is literary about literature and exclusively seeking facts, or a total identification of what is narrated with reality: "Those who only look for that indirect happiness in the reading are poor readers; but those who say that the good reader can never find pleasure in the reading are wrong" (1961, 31). Realism—or "realisms," to which Lewis devotes an entire chapter—implies the reader's reflection that "These things can happen," but it hardly requires the absolute credibility demanded of scientific books (1961, 107).

Stierle, who merits Susana Reisz de Rivarola's insightful comments (1979, 112), starts from the thesis, which I have equally adopted, that the fictional (or IFR) and the real (or EFR) are interrelated in such a way that one acts as a horizon of the other (1979, 313), regardless of the fact that the literary text may essentially consist of a series of non-verifiable assertions. But the reader does not wish to verify them anyway, nor could he in fact do so, any more than he could in the context of a large number of communicative situations in which he participates; therefore he always takes some things for granted by virtue of Grice's cooperation principle. As Stierle (1979, 300) points out, "Le texte de fiction s'efface au profit d'un au-delà textuel, d'une illusion que le récepteur—sous l'impulsion du texte—produit lui même. L'illusion (comme résultat de la réception quasi pragmatique de la fiction) est un hors-texte comparable à celui de la réception pragmatique."

Stierle's thesis is highly illuminating, and I only take exception, as I have already noted, to his negative view of the naive forms of reception. His quasi-pragmatic reading is, in fact, that of intentional realism. It begins with the *epoché* of the fictional pact, or the voluntary suspension of disbelief. Next we become increasingly involved in the represented world, we identify with the characters (in a novel or a play) or with the lyrical speaker and his emotions (in poetry), until we cease perceiving the literary discourse as an illusion-provoking mechanism, even though we begin to live the illusion precisely because of this discourse (if the discourse were not "eminent," to use Gadamer's expression, it would fail). Finally, we do not return to the epistemological attitude previous to our voluntary *epoché*. The virtuality of the text and our intentional experience of it will lead us to heighten the qualitative order of its internal world of reference until we integrate it without reservations into our own external, referential—i.e., realist—world. Therein lies the truth of literature which is, as Pablo Picasso put it (referring to the work of art in general), "a lie that makes us tumble to the truth" (cited by Harry Levin 1963, 39); a truth, moreover, that does not require our denying the autonomy of the text as an artistic construct vis-à-vis reality and the author's intentions. Realism originates in us, the readers, who appropriate this truth as a fully actualized aesthetic object, by virtue of the *non integrated epoché* that Husserl's phenomenology can easily account for. And thus, the suspension of disbelief gives way to the enthusiasm of epiphany.

But the literary text must have a formally accomplished configuration in order to overcome our initial scepticism. In other words, just as the text cannot be completely realized without a reading, the latter cannot be performed *in vacuum*. Those who attempt to oppose the aesthetics of literary reception to formalism usually forget this fact, as they also forget that the Russian formalists of the Moscow circle, being Gustav Spet's faithful students, were equally aware, as we have seen, of the Husserlian phenomenological foundation of the literary work.

Despite the intrinsically subjective character of the reading process, moreover, we need not embrace a solipsistic perspective. For example, Jeffrey Stout (1982, 4), in asking himself what the meaning of a text is, comes up at first with a predictable answer: "the author's intention and the contextual meaning"; but then he acknowledges that readers also create meaning and that they are far from doing it in a completely arbitrary manner. Of course, there is the so-called "semantic response" to a text, which we shall shortly examine. Additionally, however, "most readings are offered within *traditions*, *communities*, and *institutions* that set limits to the interests and purposes an interpretation may serve" (1982, 8).

It is Stanley E. Fish (1976), one of the most prominent American representatives of the literary response theory, who has formulated the notion of "interpretive communities" which Stout appears to invoke and which Jean E. Kennedy (1981), among others, has also taken up. For Fish, the actualizer of the text is, in a certain sense, the one who writes it, its author, so that the "interpretive communities are made up of those who share interpretive strategies not for reading (in the conventional sense) but for writing texts, for constituting their properties and assigning their intentions. In other words, these strategies exist prior to the act of reading and therefore determine the shape of what is read rather than as is usually assumed, the other way around" (Fish 1976, 483).

The practice of intentional realism represents one of these interpretive communities, and so does the opposite practice of "derealizing" or "metaliterary" reading. But I disagree with Fish when he says that these communities "are not natural or universal, but *learned*," emphasizing instead his statement that "the ability to interpret is not acquired; it is constitutive of being human" (1976, 484), which I believe also describes the spontaneous tendency toward intentional realism. I will, however, grant that, during the nineteenth century, realism not only created a school of writing, but also considerably perfected the school—or interpretive community—of intentional realist readers.

In the case of realism, then, we are dealing with a typical phenomenon of literary response, with multiple variants according to the different pragmatic circumstances accompanying it. A given period can favor the interpretive community of intentional realism, while another period can favor its opposite, not to mention the specific attitude, competence, and individual situation of each reader. Obviously, the notion of "hermeneutic distance" is of utmost importance in this regard: the contemporaneity of text and reader favors a certain identification between their two referential fields, while an actualization projected through time does not, although one need not draw the conclusion that an intentionally realist actualization would necessarily be more difficult in the second case. This vast array of possibilities, as well as the theoretization of the phenomenon itself, definitely requires a methodology of empirical analyses.

Intentional Realism and Empirical Corroboration

Roman Ingarden himself has repeatedly acknowledged in *Vom Erkennen des literarischen Kunstwerks* that the greatest problem concerning the cognition of the concretizations of a literary work of art—i.e., its critical and intersubjective apprehension as an aesthetic object—is to find a method and a descriptive metalanguage ad hoc (1968, § 28, 29, 32, 33). This problem has been addressed by a select group of pragmatically oriented semioticians and literary response theorists who, especially in Germany, have elaborated a genuinely empirical theory of literature. As Siegfried Schmidt (1978, 61) writes, "The work as 'understood' by the (majority of) recipients . . . is the field of research upon which literary scholars base their theories"—an orientation adopted not only by Schmidt (1978; 1979; 1980; 1980c; 1981), but also by Götz Wienold (1973), Rainer Warning (1979), Norbert Groeben (1981), W. Kindt (1981), and Karlheinz Stierle (1979).

Michael Rifaterre also believes that the reader's response to the text is the only causal relation that can be invoked in explaning literary phenomena (1979, 98), a quite important principle in corroborating or invalidating our hypothesis of intentional realism. We need to attempt a "methodological objectivation," as Schmidt notes, developing the "procedures of analysis, description, and explanation that permit a continuous movement from the structuring of the text to the structuring of the recipient's behavior; i.e., that involve complex communication processes about texts." And Schmidt concludes with two important observations: "This kind of task can be performed only in an interdisciplinary manner. Its difficulties should not be underestimated" (1978, 67). Schmidt's interdisciplinary approach would involve the psychology of language, social psychology, and sociology; whereas the difficulties he foresees would derive from assigning new duties to some of the most common procedures, such as interviews, surveys, field studies, etc.

W. Kindt, one of the members of the NIKOL group founded by Schmidt in 1973 at the University of Bielefeld and now located at Siegen, believes—in open opposition to his colleagues—that the new outside methods to be assimilated and practised in the context of an empirical theory of literature will never completely replace the interpretation of texts, even if understood "in a new, nontraditional sense of the word" (1981, 486). J.-K. Adams shares Kindt's opinion, arguing that a literary critic can thoroughly describe only his own response to literature, because neither the most exhaustive survey nor the most sagacious interview will allow us to objectivize what occurs second by second in a reading brain. That is why the researcher "is forced for practical and theoretical reasons, to use his own experience in the form of reading and competence as the basis for a description of the reader's experience" (1985, 31).

In our case, it is a question of confirming, correcting, or invalidating the hypothesis that a) realism is always produced by the reader; and that b) the reader, regardless of his literary competence, always tends to produce intentional realism in his actualizations of literary texts, except when he adopts a reflexive, non-empathic attitude. Our hypothesis can at least rely on the empirical experience of realist "productivity," owing to our own reading experience, during which, as Kindt has argued, our attitude is different from the one we assume in a critical, scholarly, or pedagogical interpretation. It is a matter of practicing a sort of self-splitting that would enable us to gain distance from ourselves as spontaneous readers in order to observe our own process or "act of reading." So we would go directly to Ingarden's fourth type of cognitive contact with the literary work of art (1968): the reflexive knowledge of an aesthetic concretization of the work, identifiable with the reader's experience, in which the work itself turns from an artistic object (Mukařovsky would say "artifact") into an aesthetic object; for, in Paul Ricoeur's words (1983, 117), "Le texte ne devient oeuvre que dans l'interaction entre texte et réception."

It is clear, however, that this isolated, empirical factor of an intentional realist reading will not suffice. The first recourse we obviously have is to rely on other critical readings; and the closer these readings are to the non-conventional model of explanation distanced from the actualized text, the more they can serve our purpose. In this sense, María del Carmen Bobes Naves's research would be very useful for a study of intentional realism in *La Regenta*, since it lacks neither the implicit perspective of reception and response nor the reflection of the intentional experience of the represented objectivities, especially of the characters in their idiosyncrasies, personality, and conduct. Taking into account several such readings will enrich the empirical exploration initiated by the critic doubled as reader. This is precisely what Riffaterre (1966) did, when he attempted to rebutt the "linguistic fallacy" of Roman Jakobson and Claude Lévi-Strauss's interpretation of Baudelaire's sonnet "Les chats" with the help of the theoretical concept of "arch-reader." The latter is a sort of empiricization of an ideal reader composed of Baudelaire himself (also a critic of certain concrete solutions regarding the poem's eighth line), Gautier, Laforgue, several French critics, editors, and literary historians, English translators, as well as Jakobson and Lévi-Strauss themselves. Riffaterre completes his "arch-reader" through surveys of college students and other informants.

We do not lack a certain theoretical and pragmatic tradition in the field of surveys, including such classic works as I. A. Richards's *Practical Criticism* (1929) or, in a different domain, Dauber's research, taken up by Sartre (1940, 176–177), on the accuracy of color perception in a painting within a group of nearly four hundred people. This kind of research has also produced very good results in studying certain aspects of poetry. In the case of Spanish literature, one can mention David Gitlitz's study, "Hacia una definición empírica de la aliteración" (NRFH 22, 1973, 85–90) and its application to the "map" of the semantic fields of Jorge Guillén's poetry in *Gramática de "Cántico" (Análisis semiológico)* by María del Carmen Bobes Naves (Barcelona: Planeta-Universidad de Santiago de Compostela, 1975). In the field of Spanish drama, Alfonso Sastre (1965, 183–188) conducted a survey among the audiences of several performances of Mauro Muñiz's *El tintero*, which mostly resulted in responses such as "it depicts the reality of life" or "very realistic," thus supporting our view of intentional realism. In Germany, within the domain of empirical literary theory, Schmidt (1978, 64, n. 44) mentions R. Zobel's doctoral thesis, "The Dramatic Text," which, "using experimental socio-psychological methods, investigates the audience's emotional reaction to the performance of a modern Austrian play, with 781 persons being surveyed." One can also mention, within the field of teaching methodologies, Robert de Beaugrande's research (1981) as well as that of Terry Phillips (1971) and Charles R. Cooper (1976), both conditioned by their disciplinary interest—the teaching of literature—and the theoretical approaches of David Bleich and Normand Holland, director of the Buffalo School of Psychoanalytic Criticism. From their research we can also extrapolate conclusions that favor intentional realism.

The first conclusion is provided by Cooper, who, in his classroom surveys on modes of reading, determines that school-age readers are interested in the content of a literary work, rather than in its form or style (1976, 79). Cooper's conclusion empirically validates Ingarden's argument that the layer of the represented objectivities and, to some extent, that of the aspects prevail phenomenologically over the linguistic layer, which, while supporting the other two, remains unnoticed (an argument that can equally be linked to Zola's idea of a naturalist language, thin and transparent like glass). Phillips, on the other hand, studies the responses to three short poems by twenty-four children between the ages of ten and eleven, divided into six groups. Significantly, the majority of these responses is oriented toward "presenting" and "picturing": "In a presenting response the child is presenting his own experience, something in his own life the poem reminds him of. In a picturing response the child is building up a visual image of objects, people, or places in the poem" (Phillips 1971, 56–57). Secondly, Phillips corroborates Norman Holland's theory (1968; 1973; 1975) that it is not the words of the text that determine an individual's mode of reading, but rather his "ego-style," because the reader recreates the literary work mainly in order to reconstruct his own character.

In turn, Wolfgang Iser (1975, 44) mentions Walter Homberg and Karlheinz Rossbacher's unpublished study on *Lesen auf Lande. Literarische Rezeption und Mediennutzung im ländlichen Siedlungsgebiet Salzburgs. Bericht über ein empirisches Forschungsprojekt* (1977), which sets out "to empiricize" Iser's own theory of aesthetic response. For that purpose, the authors asked a selected group of individuals who had no previous literary training to read Christoph Meckel's *Der Zünd* (1964) and then polled them on how they related the segments of the discourse in the reading process and which repertoire they used in order to interpret it. Iser's (1975, 45) assessment of the survey is significant, because he points out that the reciprocal relations between a particular theoretical model of literary reception and empirical research not only constitute an example of interdisciplinarity or exchange between human sciences, but also facilitate the practical validation of the theory.

Siegfried J. Schmidt has also employed surveys in his well-known studies of *empirischen Literaturwissenschaft*, a *Grundriss* of which he started publishing in 1980. In the preface to the issue of *Poetics* (1981) that I have already mentioned, he passionately defends their utility against those critics who consider that the unavoidable margin of error, arbitrariness, hypocrisy, or distortion on the part of the surveyed subjects invalidate their conclusions (Schmidt 1981, 328). His own experiment concerned the reception of modern narrative, with all its thematic and formal implications. In order to perform this experiment, Schmidt published five short German texts in the Bielefeld daily newspaper, *Neue*

Westfalische Zeitung, during five consecutive weekends in the fall of 1976, then passed along lengthy questionnaires to one hundred subscribers to the newspaper, two hundred students of two different levels, and one hundred workers who had taken a literature course in *Volkshochschule,* and finally processed the results together with R. Zobel in the summer of 1977. Finally, to conclude this brief overview, one can mention E. Klemenz-Belgardt's informative article (1981, 365) on the empirical theory of literary reception in the United States, which refers, for example, to H. L. Frankel's doctoral dissertation (Temple University, 1972) that surveys a number of black and white student responses to *The Adventures of Huckleberry Finn.*

The theory of intentional realism can find important empirical support in some of these surveys, as we have seen in the case of Alfonso Sastre for drama, Terry Phillips for poetry, and Charles R. Cooper in general. Anthony R. Petrosky (1976), who belongs to Norman Holland's school of research, has specifically concentrated on studying a number of students' perceptive responses to reality and fantasy in narrative and poetry through weekly recorded interviews, later transcribed by the teacher and nine students from a Buffalo junior high school. The responses of two girls particularly stand out, reflecting marked "individual styles" in their readings, to use Holland's terminology. As Petrosky explains, an "individual style is determined by how a reader perceives reality," so that "Mary Kay's style does not give much credence to reverie as a part of reality while Kathy sees reverie as an important aspect of reality" (1976, 255). The two realist intentionalities, therefore, are different, one leaning toward an objective and sensual reality, the other toward a more abstract reality, of deep meanings, involving a more open and complex vision of the world. They also confirm Antonio Risco's argument (1987, 12) that realist literature is no less conventional than fantastic literature.

Of interest here is also Ada Wildekamp, I. van Montfort, and W. van Ruiswyk's paper, read at the University of Amsterdam and then partially published in *Poetics* (1980), which is an empirical investigation of reader's response theory based on a survey of twenty-five high school and twenty-six college students of Dutch and Economics. By comparing the results of their survey to the hypotheses about fictionality that they had previously selected and organized in a coherent system, the authors find disagreements between these hypotheses and empirical proof. But, from our standpoint, the most important fact is that even after taking into consideration "the influence which level of education, discipline, and general and 'literary' knowledge exercise on the activation of the fictionality convention" (1980, 561) and the existence of effective "fictionality indicators, either of a syntactic-semantic nature or of a pragmatic nature" (1980, 561), a high percentage of the surveyed individuals "opted for 'indeterminable' when asked to judge a text on its fictionality potential" (1980, 565); in other words, they clearly opted for intentional realism.

The text, then, never offers itself as radically fictive or realist because of its intrinsic qualities, regardless of the reader's attitude—a hypothesis supported by another empirical experiment, performed by Michael Riffaterre in "L'explication des faits littéraires." Riffaterre selected a fragment from Zola's *La débacle*, in which the narrator reports the German siege of Sédan with great topographic and toponymical precision, and replaced the names of the towns and places in the Ardennes with toponyms from the Landes telephone directory. He concluded that "cette alteration de la référence au réel n'a pas menacé la mimesis du réel. Comme dit André Breton, l'imagination est ce qui tend à devenir réalité" (Riffaterre 1971, 26–27).

The kind of criticism against the methodology of the new empirical literary theory that Schmidt (1981, 328) has had to counter may be generated by our insecurity when walking the path of other disciplines that can, nevertheless, effectively cooperate with ours; moreover, literary scholarship has always required that its practitioners keep an open mind toward other disciplines. There is still much to be done before we reach the point of equilibrium between inference and empirical deduction. On the other hand, one can readily see the threat of inane arbitrariness in certain proposals that subject any theoretical principle—for example, literariness—to evaluative "re-elaborations" of the kind that J. Iwhe indulges in: "the individual $P(i)$ *is willing to give a certain value* to the linguistic expression $a(i)$, in a given moment $t(i)$, in a specific place $r(i)$, in the sociocultural context $k(i)$, and in the psyco-physic conditions $z(i)$" (S. J. Schmidt 1978, 46). A project of this sort, aimed at the empirical determination of intentional realism, would of course be completely unrewarding.

And yet the very phenomenological foundation of the theory of realism requires pragmatic corroboration. Fernando Lázaro Carreter (1969, 141) considers that this controversial and polysemious critical-literary concept can be recuperated only "if one renounces its supposed univocity, if one divides its signification into as many meanings, i.e., into as many realisms without quotation marks or italics, as necessary; into as many authors and as many works as we subject to critical scrutiny." It would perhaps be too daring to add without discrimination: "and into as many realisms as there are readers." But it would be useful to trace the grouping of readers into interpretive communities projecting a similar intentionality on literary texts until they become realist.

We shall now attempt to do, from the standpoint of the recipient, what has already been done from the standpoint of linguistic assertions and their content: to describe specific systems of sense-conferring or realist productivity in order to create an archive, as complete as possible, of empirical evidence in the understanding of a literary phenomenon that is also pragmatic. This performative program would respond to the empirical exigencies we have dealt with, but it could certainly not ignore the textual factor. Otherwise, we would fall into another fallacy—the pragmatic or receptive one—that would inhibit further progress in the study of realism. In fact, according to Wienold (as cited by Schmidt 1980c, 153), one of the main goals of empirical literary theory is to investigate the correlations between the properties of the text and its recipients' behavior, a task that has been undertaken by N. Groeben, among others (cf. Schmidt 1978, 59–65).

5

The Realist Reading

Even accepting that realism is not necessarily based on specific formal properties—just as the literariness of a text cannot be "isolated" through specific linguistic features—we can still search for the literary forms that, while not reproducing reality better than others, stimulate more intensely a realist actualization of the text to which they belong. In this sense, we would favor a poetics of realist productivity, rather than one of mimetic or genetic realism. And in the manner of Riffaterre, who through his "arch-reader" identifies the linguistic facts that prevail in the recipient's attention as authentic stylistic realities, could we perhaps empirically determine which formal units act upon the reading public, producing a realist intentionality? And would it be useful to adopt, for this purpose, Itamar Even-Zohar's concept of *realemes* (1985), understood as a full set of formal and contentual elements which can be classified in specific repertoires for each culture and which can in fact produce literary realism?

We would, therefore, need to find a new point of equilibrium between textual immanence and phenomenological actualization. Although the reader may use the text, the text can (as Gadamer and other scholars have argued) in turn appropriate the reader and affect his receptive behavior, greatly limiting the possibilities of arbitrariness if the reader performs in a normal fashion. Piero Raffa (1967, 37) makes this point in relation to Pirandello: "Therefore, in a certain way, it is we who grant meaning to the literary work. I say in a certain way, because it is not obviously true that we invent meaning according to our free will. It is not for nothing that the works possess an objective structure." Although Raffa never quotes or mentions Roman Ingarden, here he seems coincidentally to paraphrase a passage from *Das literarische Kunstwerk* (1931, § 62). In this passage, Ingarden draws a parallel between the rainbow phenomenon—which is neither "psychic" nor totally objective, but the result of a visual perception under certain empirical conditions—and the concretization of a literary work, which is an intentional experience, but whose ontological foundation is the objective existence of a text with specific features. To these features *Vom Erkennen des literarischen Kunstwerks* (1968, § 27) attributes the task of prefiguring the form of reception.

With regard to this last point, Edith Klementz-Belgardt's diagnosis (1981) is highly revealing. In her report on the American empirical studies of literary response, she points out that most of these studies have deplorably abandoned the description and analysis of the discursive properties that determine the reading of a text, and she suggests that the pragmatic applications of the concept of "implicit reader" should open the way "for generating verifiable assumptions about the role of texts in literary interactions" (1981, 375).

The Implied Reader

Indeed, the textual figure of the implied reader, derived from Wayne C. Booth's "implied author" and later developed theoretically by Wolfgang Iser (1972), is one of the principal instruments in motivating a realist reading response. Iser does not mention this aspect, however, nor does he seek empirical corroboration for his theoretical formulations. If for him a signified must clearly be the result of an interaction between the signs of the text and the reader's acts of understanding (Iser 1976, 9), then the implied reader represents one of these "textual signs," but Iser neglects its relation to the concrete acts of understanding on the part of specific readers.

I have already mentioned Iser's indeterminate position between an intrinsically immanent view and a phenomenology of reading. This indeterminacy is also present in his definition of the implied reader as a structure that "incorporates both the prestructuring of the potential meaning of the text, and the reader's actualization of this potential through the reading process" (1972, XII). Thus, Iser's implied reader is both an instance of reception inherent in the text and the phenomenal actualization of the text through an act of reading. The ambiguity can be solved by making a clear distinction between the two. On the one hand, the implied reader would be a composite of forms that are present in the text and, therefore, identifiable through an intrinsic analysis. On the other hand, we could have an empirical method, such as Riffaterre's "arch-reader," to record how these forms impact reading behaviors in one direction or another.

I am persuaded that one of the crucial elements of realist productivity in a narrative text is the configuration of a realist implied reader within this text, because a realist novel will be one that sets in motion all the internal mechanisms of textual control of the reader's response in order to guide it in a realist direction, toward a realist meaning. It should be obvious, however, that regardless of how strong the textual will to exercise control may be, the margin of hermeneutic discretion on the part of each reader or interpretive community will always remain very wide.

When we dealt with the issue of fictionality, we saw the importance that some authors accorded the instance of implicit assertion in determining the fictional status of a text (John R. Searle, 1975; Samuel R. Levin, 1976; Fernando Martínez Bonati, 1978; S. Reisz de Rivarola, 1979). Peter Rabinowitz (1977) is one of the few scholars, however, who approaches this question from the standpoint of literary reception. He suggests a theory of realism based on the distance between the "authorial" and "narrative audiences" (1971, 131–133), i.e., between the reader's actual response in relation to what the author intended this response to be and the text's own means of programming and controlling the reader's response. So, according to Rabinowitz, in most realist novels, such as *War and Peace*, readers are asked to accept very little or in many cases nothing that contradicts their main beliefs and experiences; whereas in fantastic or anti-realist novels—for example in *Alice in Wonderland*—readers are asked to assume a set of beliefs that, like the existence of the White Rabbit, contradict their daily experience of reality. Consequently, the wider the gap between the two poles, the more difficult it is for the reader to establish a bridge between them (Rabinowitz 1977, 131–132).

Rabinowitz's very useful theory of realism from the reader's perspective is marred by his use of an idiosyncratic and rather ambiguous terminology when referring to various instances of immanent and extrinsic reception of the literary text—an issue that has already caused rivers of ink to flow because of its byzantine critical treatment. When I also approached it in 1984, my purpose was to adopt a clear theoretical paradigm for each of the different levels of reception, giving them unambiguous names and adopting the most functional critical metalanguage available, thus avoiding terminological inflation. The main distinction I established then (Villanueva 1984, 344–348), which can still be useful in the present context, is that between a "represented reader" and a "non-represented" (or implied) one. Tzvetan Todorov already implies this distinction when he writes: "le rôle du lecteur, la plupart du temps, ne reste pas implicite mais se trouve réprésenté dans le texte même, sous les traits d'un personnage témoin" (1978, 57).

Indeed, the narrative rhetoric of all ages has included a dialogic play between the narrator or implied author and the reader. The latter maintains a communication with the authorial voice—or voices—that can acquire numerous overtones and respond to many functional purposes. In contrast to this reader, the non-represented, implied reader is a deeper instance, consistent with the space of activity that must be occupied for the actualization of the text to occur properly, or, as Umberto Eco (1979, 62) puts it, with the "insieme di condizioni di felicità, testualmente stabilite, che devono essere soddisfate perché un texto sia pienamente attualizzato nel suo contenito potenziale." As I pointed out in my earlier study (1984), the non-represented reader is not only equivalent to Eco's "lettore modello" and Iser's "implizite Leser," but also to Walter Gibson's "mock reader," Stanley E. Fish's "informed reader," and Erwin Wolf's "der intendierte Leser." It is an implied, fictive, competent, and programmed ideal reader, grounded in the schematic character of the literary text, which, in addition to having explicit instructions of how it should be read, produces cooperative responses from its recipients through the elements it lacks, through its gaps and indeterminacies. Both of these textual aspects, moreover, create the implied or non-represented reader as a key to understanding realist productivity or intentional realism.

Literary Forms and Realist Reception

Here I intend analyzing not how signs imitate, represent, or reproduce the author's reality, but rather how they can generate, in empirical recipients, an effect of intentional recognition of their own reality through the textual determination of a specific implied, non-represented reader. This effect is well described by the French expression, *l'effet de réel*, which has become widely used as a result of a brief but stimulating work by Roland Barthes (1968), although it originally comes, as Philippe Hamon (1973) has noted, from Champfleury's famous essay on *Le réalisme* (1857). But I am interested in realism not from the standpoint of the genetic fidelity of the text to its author's referent, but rather from the standpoint of the reader's realist response to its forms. The task of an empirical theory of literary realism would thus be to determine the objective results of the final phase of this response.

In the absence of such empirical results we need to experiment with the dialogical relation between the text and the reader's response through the reactions of the critic who, as we have seen, "splits" himself in order to be able simultaneously to observe his behavior as a reader of the text. Here Charles Grivel's *Production de l'interêt romanesque* (1973 and 1973 b) which, not unlike Hamon's study, derives a theory of realism from a vast body of nineteenth-century French texts, may be of great help, although less for its ample empirical documentation than for its theoretical content. For Grivel "le texte est son effet, son effet le contient" so that the text "se mesure par son activité, par ce qu'il est susceptible de produire" (1973, 17). Because it produces its own reading, the text "commande la (les) lecture(s) correcte(s) qui est (sont) susceptible(s) d'être faite(s) de lui même" (1973, 26), for which purpose it has, as a "rôle du roman," the reader "prévu par le texte" (1973, 96), i.e., our implied, non-represented reader. Grivel's view is thus another version of what Manfred Naumann called *Rezeptionsvorgabe*, or "structured prefiguration" (cf. Iser 1976, 36).

Pointing in the same direction, Marcello La Matina, in the wake of Umberto Eco, considers realism to be mainly a pragmatic issue: "Costruire un testo realista significa invece costruire un dispositivo testuale capace di produrre e di far riconoscere delle individualitá. *Il testo realista é una macchina che produce delle ecceità testuali.*" By *ecceità* La Matina understands a "funzione indicale" through which "il sistema della enunziazione narrativa entra in rapporto con oggetti particolari del nostro mondo di riferimento" (1985, 82). In this sense, La Matina confirms Lázaro Carreter's characterization of realism as a dynamic principle within a literary series (1969, 141), because realism depends, to a large extent, on the writer's ability to find new techniques of producing realist readings among his contemporary recipients. If the writer assumes that realism is an effect to be induced in the reader through an ad hoc prefiguration of an implied non-represented reader, his audience's fluctuating expectations dictate his continuous search for new compositional and stylistic possibilities. In this sense, the "reality effect" generates a perpetual dynamic of literary forms.

One can then elaborate repertoires of realist forms, as has in fact been done for a long time, for these forms are realistic not because they closely reproduce reality by directly linking the discourse to the referent, but because of the ways in which they configure an implied non-represented reader, guiding the empirical reader toward intentional realism. Describing and classifying forms will be of use to us, therefore, only if we reverse the direction of their study: not from the referent to the text, but from the text to the reader and his context.

Ángel Tarrío (1979, 216) has already suggested the need for a "theoretical model that would include a minimum of rules enabling a language to induce a reading that we would call realist." Such a model can be found in rhetoric, and is not very far from ours, because as Grivel (1973, 29) reminds us, "toute Rhétorique est Rhétorique de l'effet." To the rhetoricians, the mimetic intention was crucial in attributing poetic (or, in modern terms, literary) status to an opus, for it does not appear in forensic and deliberative discourse. The object of imitation is the reality of life, condensed in the opus as a true *mimema*, according to the principle of instantaneous and essential totality or *kazolou* (it would be interesting to relate old principles such as this one with modern concepts, such as the Marxist notions of the typical and the particular—*das Besondere*—in which the individual and the general coincide, giving birth to the total essence—*das Wesen*—of the represented reality). Specific procedures were devised to this effect (cf. Heinrich Lausberg 1960, 11, 445–449) such as *sermocinatio, laus, descriptio, fictio personae, metaphora, allegoria*, and especially *evidentia*—or the Greek *hypotiposis*—a term that, according to Quintilian, Celsus defined as a figure that is crucial for the *effet de réel*, bringing before the reader's eyes—if that were possible—things or events in all their details, just as though one were contemplating them. Luisa López Grijera (1986), for example, has studied the use of this procedure by the great Spanish realists of the Golden Age.

Clara Reeve (1785, I. 111) implicitly provides a similar repertoire of procedures when she defines the romance and the novel by contrast, including considerations of effect and response: "The Romance is an heroic fable, which treats of fabulous persons and things.—The Novel is a picture of real life and manners, and of the times in which it is written. The Romance, in lofty and elevated language, describes what never happened nor is likely to happen. The Novel gives a familiar relation of such things, as pass every day before our eyes, such as may happen to our friend, or to ourselves; and the perfection of it, is to represent every scene, in so easy and natural manner, and to make them appear so probable, as to deceive us into a persuasion (at least while we are reading) that all is real, until we are affected by the joys or distresses, of the persons in the story, as if they were our own."

In turn, George J. Becker (1963, 23–32) begins his anthology of documents on literary realism by explicitly spelling out its main rules: a choice of contemporary and common topics

that can be attributed to a detailed, apparently nonselective, observation of reality, including all kinds of materials—even those that are not only vulgar but also degrading and obscene, because sincerity and respect for the facts is of utmost importance in the artistic accomplishment of realism. In the specific field of literary forms, Becker points out the technique of the *tranche de vie* (slice-of-life), subsequently leading to the demise of the traditional concept of the hero or protagonist and to the method of "authorial self-effacement," favoring documentation and observation as a source of certainty for the narrative.

But the most important contribution in this regard is that of Philippe Hamon (1973), to which he has added a more recent article (1985) as well as a book on literary description (1981) that includes materials previously published as articles (1972 and 1980). In his 1972 study, Hamon wanted to isolate, from the textual practice of nineteenth-century realism and naturalism, a series of formal and thematic features of realist discourse, not from the exclusive perspective of the literary assertion, but considering the process of assertion as a whole, i.e., investigating "la relation entre le programme d'un auteur et un certain statut de lecteur à créer" (Hamon 1973, 421). Such a "poetics" of realism would be grounded in a true pragmatics, replacing the classic question, "How does literature copy reality?" with "How does literature make us believe that it copies reality?" In other words, what stylistic means and what mandatory structures does literature consciously or unconsciously bring into play in order to create the special status of a "realist" reader?

Regrettably, however, this promising program, so close to that of intentional realism, remains unfulfilled, because Hamon, instead of making the qualitative move from the text to its reception, confines himself to the relations between the text and the reality from which it starts, through the author. So not only does he tacitly conform to Auerbach's characterization of realism (Hamon 1973, 418, n. 16), but also ends up with a pragmatic description of the realist communicative process that leans entirely toward the genetic, rather than the receptive, side. Hamon thus operates on the following assump-

tions: "1) le monde est *riche*, divers, froissonnant, discontinu, etc.; 2) je peux *transmettre une information* au sujet de ce monde; 3) la langue peut *copier* le réel; 4) la langue est *seconde* par rapport au réel (elle l'exprime, elle ne la crée pas, elle lui est 'extérieure'); 5) le *support* (le message) doit s'effacer au maximum; 6) le *geste* producteur du message (style) doit s'effacer au maximum; 7) mon lecteur doit croire a la *vérité* de mon information sur le monde; etc." (1973, 422).

Hamon's later characterization of realist discourse as a *discours contraint*, hedged by a large number of pressures and determinants according to two main principles, *lisibilité* and *description* (1973, 445 and 442), is quite accurate, but it leaves untouched the exploration of the effects of literary forms. This exploration is precisely what concerns me (as well as Ángel Tarrío—1976; 1979), because all of the compositional and stylistic devices that a realist discourse puts into play and Hamon has studied create a certain implied reader—a key figure in projecting intentional realism within the text. Consequently, the elements isolated by Hamon, along with those provided by Grivel and others, are veins to be explored by means of empirical procedures that condition the reader's behavior through their effective performance. Charles Grivel, moreover, does adopt a pragmatic perspective of the text in his magnum opus (1973), amply supported by a companion volume (1973b). Already in the title of his work, Grivel refers to the genesis of an interest that "se produit comme déchiffrement . . . *il n'est d'intérêt romanesque que ce déchiffrement*" (1973, 90); and this deciphering, in the literature that Grivel deals with, is essentially of a realist nature. He also adds (1973, 256): "*La 'réalité' (l'effet de réalité) est un produit de l'activité textuelle, singulièrement du roman.*" This is why Grivel's contribution is of key importance for an updated study of intentional realism.

Hamon's principle of *lisibilité*, which C. Duchet (1973) supports in general terms, can be related to the well-known passage on language, in Zola's "Les romanciers naturalistes," that I have cited in relation to genetic realism, because it demands a sort of "non-style"—always in prose, Hamon (1973, 418) emphasizes—a literary language as clean and transparent as crystal. In terms of intentional realism, this non-style projects an implied reader who needs to make no hermeneutical effort with language (as opposed, say, to Baroque discourse, which constantly demands such effort by means of irony, parody, oxymoron, metaphor, or symbol) and, therefore, is free to concentrate on the level of represented objectivities in the text. In this respect, Ángel Tarrío (1979, 213) speaks of the "abandonment of the reader"—abandonment, one should add, of the empirical reader in order to stimulate the implied, non-represented reader projected by Hamon's "non-style text."

The principle of legibility tends, by stylistic and other means, to avoid any "static" (in the sense of communication theory) that may interfere with the process of transmitting information at all costs, which accounts for the predictability of the majority of the contentual elements, that "banalité des choses décrites" parallel to the banality "des mondes de présentation" admirably studied by Françoise van Rossum-Guyon (1970, 113) in relation to Butor's *La modification*. Legibility, as Roman Jakobson has also pointed out, favors redundancy, anaphorism, the resolution of ambiguity, including flashbacks—"le texte renvoie à son dejà-dit" (Hamon 1973, 424)—and the mimeticism of scientific discourse, so useful because of its monosemantic virtuality, as well as the detailed psychological justification of the characters' behavior, who otherwise are preferably simple ("rectilinear" in Unamuno's words, "flat" in Forster's).

In our terms, this means a drastic reduction of the textual gaps of indeterminacy, to the extent that such a reduction is at all possible, bringing textual schematism to a point where the cooperative reader can easily fill it in and confer full meaning upon it. It would also be easy to verify the principle of legibility by means of surveys that would empirically record the responses of real readers to the prescriptions projected by an implicit, non-represented reader. One would thus dispense with the metaliterary game, which greatly complicates everything that refers to the instance of the immanent reception of the text, ignoring the inevitable "neutralisation ou . . . *détonalisation* du message" (Hamon 1973, 434). Here one can recall Gérard Genette's precise formula (1972, 187): "la mimésis se définissant par un maximum d'information et un minimum d'informateur, la diégesis par le rapport inverse."

Hamon himself (1973, 425) mentions one more feature of this "constrained" realist discourse: "le récit est embrayé sur une méga (extra) Histoire" or "histoire parallèle," which "en filigrane, le double, l'éclaire, le prédétermine." From the viewpoint of a phenomenology and pragmatics of realism, this would mean that the text preconditions the reader's imaginative projection of the IFR upon the EFR, which is necessarily wider and can only derive from the horizon of the actualizing subject. Therefore, as I have argued earlier, in literary realism the *hors text* is at least as important as what is in the text, because it is something that the discourse lacks but nevertheless occasions through the sum of its lacunae, thus contributing to the configuration of an implied reader.

In order to reduce the vastness of the *hors texte* and to program a less complex actualization than the one just described, one has what Hamon (1973, 427) calls the *surcodage* of the realist discourse, through visual aids, such as engravings, pictures, drawings, diagrams, etc. According to Hamon (1973, 426), the proper names of the characters as well as those of historical or geographic places and their "motivation systématique" act in the manner of citations in a pedagogic discourse, i.e., as arguments from authority that anchor the fictional world in an external objectivity and guarantee a frequently enhanced reality-effect—regardless of the real or imaginary nature of such toponyms and anthroponyms, as Michael Riffaterre's experiment (1971) shows. Morse Peckham (1970, 103) equally notes that, in a novel, the statement that the Empire State Building is "at the corner of Fifth Avenue and 34th street" or "at the corner of Madison and 72nd" produces an identical effect of referential precision—and reality—upon the reader. Françoise Gaillard (1984, 765) offers the same argument in relation to the historical novel, which produces a realistic effect on those readers who cannot verify the information provided by the fictional text. According to Gaillard, the realist representation resembles the real not because reality is its referent, but because it is its product.

Ian Watt (1957, 18) has related the novelistic accuracy of proper names with a new philosophical horizon that arose in the wake of Descartes, Locke, Berkeley, Hume, and others, in which defining the individual personality and its identity becomes more important than ever before. This particularism is reinforced by rooting the individual—or, in the novel, the character—in a specific, accurately identified, place and, above all, time. Watt (1957, 21) notes, for example, that "The 'principle of individuation' accepted by Locke was that of existence at the particular locus in space and time," and that the modern novel did not fail to be influenced by this new epistemological attitude. Grivel refers to the same attitude when he asserts that a narrative requires spatial and chronological specificity if it is to rise, develop, and support itself as a closed, sufficient, and consistent world: "Il doit dire quand, il doit dire où (qui, quoi). L'événement narratif ne se propose que muni de toutes ses coordonnées" (1973, 102). These spatial and chronological coordinates, of course, produce a reality effect: "L'historicité est cette valeur—fausse—que la fiction se donne par le biais de la temporalité. Toute marque de temporalité *authentifie*" (1973, 100). Grivel insists that *"la localisation produit la veracité du texte.* Les traits constitutifs de la localisation, initiale et continue, du texte répondent de la nécessité de celui-ci de se donner pour vrai . . . La localisation procure (conjoinement) la vraisemblance du texte; elle l'institue (conjointement) 'réalité'." It is the elements of full ontological presence, as opposed to the gaps of indeterminacy which their absence would leave behind, that construct the implicit reader of the realist discourse, the one in whom, according to Grivel (1973, 245), *"tout converge à l'édification de la véracité du texte."* In this regard, the novel is "un système de vérité, véritable pullulement de marques de vrai . . . protestation continuée de sa référentialité et vérification narrative de cette protestation."

It would be relatively easy to set up *ex profeso* questionnaires to test empirically if toponymic and anthroponymic specificity does indeed increase the reality effect of a fictional world and, if so, with what particular groups of readers. One could therefore test the effectiveness of Even-Zohar's concept of *realemes*, a very useful theoretical tool for a pragmatic theory of realism.

Description

Description is the other principle (along with *lisibilité*) of Hamon's theory of the *discours contraint* (1973, 422). The program of actualization of a realist discourse is based on the conviction that the world can be described and that all of its components, even the tiniest ones, can be defined. Indeed, according to Roland Barthes (1968), the effectiveness of realist literature largely depends on collecting minute details. María del Carmen Bobes Naves (1985, 100–101) makes the same point when she considers the impact of this predilection for details on the physical and psychological makeup of the characters in *La Regenta*.

Hamon's theory of description (1972, 467) contains an interesting observation from the standpoint of immanent reception and its possible empirical verification *a posteriori*, namely that the reader must perceive description not as the novelist's *knowledge* (or "index card") but as the characters's sharpness of vision, their *ability to see*. But here again, Hamon fails to move in the direction of a pragmatics of realist effect, preferring the framework of formal realism even as he points out its flaws: "L'attitude réaliste repose donc sur une illusion linguistique, celle d'une langue monopolisée par sa seule fonction référentielle, dans laquelle les signes seraient les analogues adéquats des choses, une grille transparent redoublant le discontinu du réel" (1972, 485).

Another important observation in Hamon's 1972 article, defining realist discourse even more precisely than before, becomes the main thesis of his later book on description (1985); namely that, because realist description contributes an "empty theme," suspending the narrative proper and replacing referentiality with some kind of continuous anaphora—"au lieu de citer le réel ('choses', 'événements') il se cite lui-même perpétuellement," (1982, 485). The realist "theme" is essentially a "deconcretization" of the signified (1985, 499), a sort of "non-theme" or negative one, which nevertheless must be appreciated as *real* by the readers (cf. also Mukařovsy 1936, 34).

Reality Effect and Authenticating Authority

Hamon also establishes a link between descriptive detail and the reality effect as follows: "L'effet de réel passerait donc essentiellement par un effet d'authorité; et l'effet d'authorité ne passe peut-être que par un effet de [la] cohérence . . . interne de l'oeuvre pour provoquer l'effet de réel." This statement refers to two important factors, one belonging to the theory of narrative assertions and the other to hermeneutics. The narrative factor is equally mentioned by Bakhtin (1989, 80), according to whom the novel is a multi-stylistic, multilingual, and multivocal phenomenon that can be divided and analyzed into several types of stylistic and compositional units, such as: 1) the author's direct narrative in all its variants; 2) the stylization of different forms of the oral narrative that the Russian formalists called *skaz*; 3) the stylization of different forms of written, semi-literary narrative, such as letters, diaries, reports, etc.; 4) several forms of authorial extra-artistic language, such as arguments, warnings, digressions, declarations, etc.; and 5) the language of the characters, stylistically individualized. From a pragmatic standpoint, all of these stylistic and compositional units can be considered *realemes*. In fact, literary critics have emphasized the importance, for realism, of a wide use of social dialects as reflected in the principle of *decorum*, according to which the author should present his characters' speech in keeping with their social status.

The other factor that is essential in achieving a realist discourse is the grounding of this discourse in a credible authority who can earn the empirical reader's confidence. Thus, what Wayne Booth calls a "reliable narrator" is crucial in configuring a realist implied reader within the text itself. Laurent Danon-Boileau (1982), in his book on "producing the fictive," also emphasizes the realist process by which readers assume not only the vision of the world but also the language of the author, who speaks to them from inside the narrative text. In turn, we have seen that Peter J. Rabinowitz (1977, 131) elaborates a theory of realism based on the distance between the authorial assertion and the audience's response. This issue has also been raised in relation to fictionality in "speech acts" theory. For example, Lubomir Dolezel, who has linked the ability of literary fictions to construct possible worlds with Austin's theory of performative speech acts, reiterates that in the particular case of narrative texts "the force of authentication is assigned to the speech acts originating with the so-called narrator. The narrator's authority to issue authenticating speech acts is given by the conventions of the narrative genre" (Doležel 1988, 490).

Here Charles Dickens's *Bleak House* (published between 1852 and 1853) provides an ironic illustration of narrative authenticating authority. In this novel, praised as one of Dickens's greatest realist achievements, a secondary character, Mr. Krook, whose intervention in the plot is over and whose life, therefore, becomes superfluous in the fictional world of the text, is simply removed from it through death by internal combustion. And in order to justify the mound of ashes that Mr. Krook leaves behind, the narrator uses an authenticating device that should sit well with those readers who share the positivist scientism common in Dickens's age: he cites similar cases of internal combustion allegedly analyzed in the sixth volume of an apocryphal *Philosophical Transactions*. This is why John W. Kronik (1988), an excellent critic of Spanish realism, emphasizes the decisive role of authorial mediation in stimulating the reader's imagination, so that he may establish the most appropriate relations, from the standpoint of realist productivity, between what is narrated and external reality.

Grivel's extensive and solid research also provides excellent insights here: all narrative situations, in addition to time, space, and characters, involve a narrative source. As Grivel notes, "Ce qui se conte a besoin, pour être narré, qu'un organe (figuré ou non) le parle" (1973, 152), whether we call it narrator or implied author, depending on the appropriate narrative situation: the narrator "*doit être considéré comme procedé scrip-*

turaire permettant la réalisation de la verité du discours romanesque" (1973, 154); whereas the author is *"le sujet de la narration métamorphosé par le fait qu'il s'est inclus dans le système de la narration; il n'est rien ni personne, mais la possibilitè de permutation de S [sujet de la narration] à D [son destinataire], de l'histoire au discours et du discours à l'histoire. Il devient un anonymat, une absence, un blanc, pour permettre à la structure d'exister comme telle"* (1973, 157).

But, in order to create a reality effect, the narrative structure must rely not only on trustworthy assertions, but also on a strict principle of internal coherence for all its elements, of which the reader will be both witness and judge. As Hamon (1985, 503) notes in his book on description, *"l'effet de réel n'est que la conséquence de la perception d'un effet de structure, réinterprété lui-même comme effet d'autorité. La croyance à l'existence des faits relatés passe non pas par la connaissance de ces faits, mais par la créance (le crédit) que le lecteur attache à tout structurateur de faits, l'auteur absent qu'il déduit de la structure même du texte."* Readers lend this "credit" by virtue of the hermeneutic principle that Gadamer (1965, 261) calls the "fore-conception of completion," which Hans Robert Jauss has brought even closer to our topic in his essay on "La perfection, fascination de l'imaginaire" (1985). According to Gadamer, this principle says that "only what really constitutes a unity of meaning is intelligible. So when we read a text we always follow this complete presupposition of completion, and only when it proves inadequate, i.e., the text is not intelligible, do we start to doubt the transmitted text and seek to discover in what way it can be remedied" (1965, 261).

In view of this principle, we can conclude that any empirical survey designed to record specific readers' perceptions of the inner coherence of a literary discourse that generates a reality effect would contribute to the empirical corroboration of intentional realism.

Realism and Paratextuality

The foregoing discussion highlights the crucial role that the beginning of a text plays in the realist productivity of a literary work. By the "beginning of a text," moreover, one should understand not only its first page or pages, but also its title—the first element of the *paratext*, to use Gérard Genette's terminology (1987). Through this paratext, present both in the *incipit* and in the title itself, we can create a "horizon of realist expectation" that will immediately produce an effect in the reader (Hamon 1973, 434).

Roman Ingarden (1931) already refers to these two paratextual elements when he comments on the logical nature of the propositions contained in Thomas Mann's titles (1931, § 25); and when, in his second treatise (1968, 256–257), he explains "the semblance of an individual reality" in the characters, objects, and events of *Buddenbrook* as an impression transmitted to the reader, from the first chapters, through certain stylistic procedures, especially through the predominance of nouns and adjectives over verbs. These procedures help, from the very beginning, to project an implied reader of realist intentionality within Mann's text.

As Gadamer argues in relation to the "hermeneutic circle and the problem of prejudices" (1965, 235 ff.), the understanding of a text is based on previous concepts that the text itself ratifies or rectifies. These "prejudices" (which for Gadamer do not have the derogatory connotations that eighteenth-century rationalism has rendered common), despite their obvious extratextual dimensions—the reader's ideology, intellectual education, and aesthetics, as well as the reader's knowledge about the author, the work, the literary movement, etc.—are in fact concentrated *immanently* in the work's title, first paragraph, first page, and first chapter. It is here that the implied reader, who attempts to direct the real reader's hermeneutic behavior, is programmed.

Grivel (1973, 166 ff.) is the first to devote a whole chapter to the "Puissance du titre," understanding that the title is the first sentence of a text, comprising the entire work. For him, "*le titre, c'est créer un intérêt, une attente, c'est promettre au lecteur d'y satisfaire.*" He is also the first to propose a "semiology of the title," then developed by his disciple Leo H. Hoek (1980), who studies the relation between the title and the work—or the *co-texte*—as a dialogue between the two.

Serge Doubrovsky (1971, 156) has also analyzed the first sentence of *A la recherche du temps perdu*, assuming that it possesses "une *capacité générative*, inconnue du langage ordinaire, et impliquant, en quelque sorte, un principe d'autogenèse du texte," programming a certain reading of it, although Doubrovsky does not explicitly say so. In the debate following Dubrovsky's paper, Henri Mitterand argues that, for the reader who receives and opens the book, the title is really the first sentence in the linguistic sense of the term (Doubrovsky 1971, 194), suggesting that one should also study the relationships between the title and the opening sentence of a text.

Finally, Jacques Dubois (1973) has analyzed the beginnings of the twenty novels included in *Les Rougon-Macquart* cycle, which, according to him, have mainly two objectives: to set in motion the "internal field of reference" and to establish the authenticity of the discourse, "en faisant référence à un hors-texte et en masquant le caractère fictif de son geste initial" (1973, 491). To this end, it is quite common, for example in the Goncourt brothers, that the first page should take the form of a dialogue, delaying the unveiling of the basic narrative assertion; but Zola prefers instead to designate a character by his or her proper name or alias "comme si ce personnage était connu de toujours et ne demandait pas à être présenté" (1973, 493). Likewise, Dubois signals the presence of descriptions and insignificant details in the first few pages of Zola's novels, a presence that, as we have seen, is conducive to a reality effect. Everything points to the creation of an implicit reader conforming to such an effect, and this reader may, from the very beginning of the text, provide the empirical reader with "unquestionable proofs of certainty," to use Juan Miguel Company-Ramón's phrase (1986, 69).

Thus, an empirically verifiable pragmatics of intentional realism can use the title, the first paragraph, and the opening chapter of a work as basic texts for gauging the reader's response to the work's structural and stylistic features geared toward a realist productivity. And through other survey techniques it would be possible to detect the prejudices, in Gadamer's hermeneutically positive sense, on which these readers's actualizations of the work are based—whether their prejudices are of a literary type, such as their reading competence and the other factors I have already mentioned, or of a wider scope: prejudices of world outlook or *ideological* ones (cf. Ángel Tarrío 1976, 59–61). By combining both survey methods we would be able to determine the pragmatics of realist productivity in any given literary text.

Intentional Realism and Poetry

The consideration of intentional realist productivity must adapt itself to the widely different pragmatic conditions within various literary genres. The novel is undoubtedly the genre in which the most ground has been covered from this standpoint, because it is usually viewed as the archetype of literary realism, so much so that theatrical realism is often associated with it; and certainly there is plenty of evidence for such an association, e.g., in Strindberg's preface to *Miss Julie*, cited by Becker (1963, 402), which shows the playwright's fondness for the Goncourt brothers.

The great "density of signs" characteristic of the theater, as well as the fact that most of these signs have considerable iconic strength, has led some scholars—even those most sceptic about realism, such as the "conventionalist" Murray Krieger—to acknowledge that in drama there is "in the most graphically immediate sense . . . an imitation of history—of history that is, as empirical reality" (Krieger 1974, 343); and this not only between 1870 and 1920, when European drama generally adopted a realist practice. But there are opposite views (with which I find it hard to agree) such as Jovan Hristič's, for whom realist theater is a hybrid form that results from bringing novelistic art onto the stage. This mixture is congenital in narrative, but alien to drama, "a genre destined for purity" (Hristič 1977, 313), which explains the attraction that great poets have always had for the theater. Hristič concludes that "drama by its nature is a nonrealistic genre" (1977, 315) which, when subjected to mimetic fidelity, limits its horizons to the paradoxical point of giving up being art and turning into mere life.

I certainly acknowledge the complexity of the theatrical phenomenon and the specificity of the pragmatic framework in which it occurs (and which determines its literariness in a greater degree than that of other genres): these conditions would require an exhaustive treatment of the possibilities and limits of intentional realism in drama that I cannot undertake here. But let me at least suggest another audacious conjecture: that the theater is paradoxically the most anti-realistic form, because the physical presence of the audience and its contact with the actors who impersonate the characters, together with all the other systems of signs placed in the service of referential illusion, produce the opposite effect of artificiality and lack of realism. One could, moreover, add that in the case of drama, in contrast to the internal process of reading, the *epoché* or fictional pact ceases to operate as soon as the public ceremony of the performance is over, the lights come on, the actors and actresses take a bow and are cheered (or booed), and the audience leaves the theater commenting on the perfection or precariousness of the performance, rather than on its intentional realist projection.

On the contrary, in poetry, the theory of intentional realism is on solid ground, even though, at first sight, this statement might be regarded as a risky paradox, since I am going against a common opinion as old as Aristotle (whose *Poetics*, however, does not exclude poetry from *mimesis*; rather, it simply does not pay much attention to it). Here I am specifically referring to the place of lyrical poetry within the spectrum of realist productivity, leaving out "certain texts—usually known as 'hermetic' or 'absurd'—which do not have any claims of coherence in reference or predication, and which, consequently, do not 'mime,' represent, or recall any conceptual plan of organization of experiential complexes" (Reisz de Rivarola 1979, 165). (Examples include what Jespersen calls *glosolalia* and Alfonso Reyes, *jitanjáforas*: a literary discourse with no specific referent and, therefore, of difficult semantic determination.)

It was Roman Ingarden (1931, § 25a) who, in his polemic with Käte Hamburger (and in part with Emil Staiger), argued incidentally that poetry was no less "mimetic" than the novel or the theater (if Jakobson never fully developed this argument, it was not because of lack of interest or ability, seeing that his classes of literary theory at the University of Lemberg were based on Rilke's poetry). Despite the obviously non-representative character of external, physical, and objectifiable referents of most poetic productions in comparison to other genres, there is a very strong intentional realism in poetry.

One could also cite Jean Paul Sartre's well-known position (1948, 48–49): poetry leans toward the non-referential—and thus "non-realistic"—arts, because the poet refuses to use language in order to name the world. He regards the word as a reality in itself, as a thing and not a sign, and does not sacrifice it in favor of the reality that it can name: "The man who speaks is beyond words, close to the object; the poet is closer to the word." Shortly before Sartre, however, the Spanish poet and critic Pedro Salinas fervently defends the relationship between poetry and reality in his book, *Reality and the Poet in Spanish Poetry* (1940). For Salinas, "if one seriously considers the poetic task . . . one reaches the conclusion that the poet, instead of remaining comfortably outside the world, lives at its very core" (1940, 185), because "the subject of poetry is the whole world. Total reality" (1940, 15); in other words, poetry takes as its subject all human psychological, natural, or material productions, as well as all human actions and culture.

Salinas's view, so radically different from Sartre's, has not remained without echo in recent years. In Spanish criticism, María del Carmen Bobes Naves has written about the "essential realism" of Jorge Guillén's poetry, relating it to phenomenology (1975, 131 ff.). Armando Plebe (1969, 137), in his book on contemporary Soviet aesthetics, mentions a tendency, for instance in Soatov's 1965 study, to redeem poetry for socialist realism because it accurately expresses the link between reality and the artist's ideals. Similarly, one can even encounter defenses of the physical or psychological mimetic nature of poetry in a genetic realist sense (of little interest to us, however). Thus, Shimon Sandbank (1985) advocates the recognition of pure referentiality in what he calls "object-poetry," which reacts against Romantic imaginarism and fantasy. To illustrate his point, he mentions concrete poems by Williams and Rilke, as well as writing techniques—generally of an iconic-visual or iconic-auditive nature—that make the lyric discourse referential. John Reichert (1981, 57) also cites assertional poems that can be read as non-fictional propositions, seriously formulated and intended by poets such as Emily Dickinson, whose work the critic considers "a treasure store of such propositional, affirmative poems," and occasionally Shakespeare, Frost, and Stevens.

From our perspective, "affirmative" poems are the ones that, because of their concentrated and essential character, being neither descriptive nor extensively developed, can obviate the schematism of the literary work of art; so they can convey a simple and pure emotion, intentionally projected by the poet from his real or imagined experience into words, and cointentionally recreated by the reader from his own experiences through an intimate assumption of the verbal message. This is when we can say, with Ortega y Gasset, that every poet plagiarizes us or, with Novalis, that poetry is the only absolute reality, so that the more poetic a discourse is, the more true it becomes:

> Die Poesie ist das echt
> absolute reelle. Dies ist der kern
> meiner Philosophie.
> Je poetischer, je wahrer.

In a sense, this poetic statement goes against one of the most common views in modern criticism, according to which the reader experiences a poem by "reviving" the poet's intimate moment in the instant of creation. My own view takes us exactly in the opposite direction: the reading process of a lyrical text produces in its immediate recipient an experience that may or may not coincide intentionally with the author's. The Portuguese poet Fernando Pessoa has written a poem entitled "Autopsicografía" (published in *Presença* in October 1932 and later included in the first volume of his *Obras completas*), which is usually cited as an example of the emotional antireality of the poem, but which in the second and third stanzas, generally ignored, accurately describes the intentional realist process that occurs in poetry:

> O poeta é um fingidor.
> Finge tão completamente
> Que chega a fingir que é dor
> A dor que deveras sente.
>
> E os que lêem o que escreve,
> Na dor lida sentem bem,
> Não as duas que ele teve,
> Mais só a que eles não têm.
>
> E assim nas calhas de roda
> Gira, a entreter a razão,
> Esse comboio de corda
> que se chama coração.

[The poet is a pretender./ He pretends so completely,/ that he even pretends that it is grief/ the grief which he really feels.// And those who read him/ feel in the grief they are reading about/ not his two griefs/ but the one that they don't feel.// And thus on circular tracks/ distracting reason turns round and round/ this toy train/ called heart.]

The *coraçao* (heart) of the last line is the meeting point of the author's and the reader's fictionality, because the *dor* (grief) to which the poet refers in the second stanza is not so much a double grief, experienced in reality and *pretended* in the text, but rather one that the readers may feel within their horizon, even if they need not experience it.

Likewise, Paul Valéry, in a prose text that Dominique Combe (1985, 35) presents as a crucial theoretical document for a phenomenology of reading, implies that poetry can be the most realist literary form, because it facilitates an intense identification between the emotion it represents and the reader's experience. "Le poème," Valery writes, "exige de nous une participation qui est plus proche de l'action complète, cependant que le conte et le roman nous transforment plutôt en sujets du rêve et de notre faculté d'être hallucinés." For

Combe (1985, 37), this means that poetry opens a referential horizon toward the reader, while narrative encloses this referential horizon within its own imaginary world. This is why, Combe says, fiction can be seen as "self-referential" and poetry as referential.

Barbara Hernstein Smith (1971, 277) similarly believes that the reader constitutes the real meaning of a poem through "an interpretation that infers from it and provides for it an appropriately rich, subtle, and coherent context of human feelings." In Spain, Carlos Bousoño (1962, I) defines a "real" communication as a variable degree of coincidence between the psychic, affective-sensitive-conceptual contents presented by the poet and those projected in the act of reading by the recipient. To this I have already referred as "cointentional realism," which I believe is intensely operative in lyric poetry. There are many empirical confirmations of this belief. For example, Anthony R. Petrosky (1976, 251–252), in his study of school children's literary perception of reality and fantasy, mentions how, upon reading Genevieve Taggard's "Millions of strawberries," his informant Kathy "recalls a childhood experience similar to the one described in the poem."

R. G. Collingwood's theory of "sympathetic understanding," frequently mentioned by Karl R. Popper and Hans Georg Gadamer, would have some points in common with cointentional convergence, except that this theory implies a certain degree of alienation on the part of the recipient from the situation and experiences of those he wishes to identify with. Gadamer's concept of aesthetic experience (1965, 63) seems, however, more closely related to it: "The work of art would seem almost by definition to become an aesthetic exprerience: that means, however, that it suddenly takes the person experiencing it out of the context of his life, by the power of the work of art, and yet relates him back to the whole of his existence." In the conclusion of his *Wahrheit und Methode*, Gadamer applies the hermeneutical principle of the "fusion of horizons" to "eminent texts," i.e., to literature, with certain nuances that are exactly the ones I have suggested regarding the functioning of intentional realism in poetry, commonly seen as an essentially "non-mimetic" genre. For example,

Gadamer says: "What I have described as a fusion of horizons is the manner in which this union (of meaning between the work and its effect) is realized, which does not allow the interpreter to speak of an original meaning of a work without his own meaning having already been introduced in the understanding of this work" (H. G. Gadamer 1965, 489). Perhaps the best illustration of what Gadamer means here is the first sonnet of Petrarch's *Canzoniere*, in which the poet, through a marked perlocutionary structure (especially in the first two stanzas), asks for the cointentional response of those who, having experienced the affections of love as he has, can understand his ravings without needing to forgive them:

> Voi ch'ascoltate in rime sparse il suono
> di quei sospiri ond'io nudriva'l core
> in sul mio primo giovenile errore
> quand'era in parte altr'uom da quel ch'io sono,
>
> del vario stile in ch'io piango e ragiono
> fra le vane speranze e'l van dolore,
> ove sia chi per prova intenda amore,
> spero trovar pietà, non che perdono.

Conclusion

Is the problem of realism a pseudo-problem? To this question, which Morse Peckham (1970) asks with a certain provocative intent, I have given a negative reply. I believe, on the contrary, that realism is one of the central issues of literary theory, because as much as we may be interested in knowing how literature works in itself, with the aid of scientific, analytical tools that are highly reliable in determining its forms or its literariness, we cannot ignore the evidence that *eminent texts* impinge upon reality, our reality. Moreover, literary works are eminent—as Gadamer (1965, 490) argues—because the "disappearance" within them of an immediate reference to reality opens them to "a certain receptive sensibility of both today and tomorrow"; they "go on speaking." The question of realism, then, is not a trivial one; on the contrary, it lies at the very core of humanism. This is why E. B. Greenwood (1962, 96), in reflecting on René Wellek's concept of realism, advocates a perfectly balanced understanding of art from both an immanent and a transcendental perspective: "Art is a world of forms and devices, but of forms and devices designed to mediate a qualitative and synthetic (as opposed to a quantitative and analytic) apprehension of life."

Peckham is right, on the other hand, that we can no longer accept an essential realism, understood as a faithful and transparent reproduction by artistic means of a fully present and univocal reality which the poet observes and out of which he creates his work—an aesthetic version of Ludovico Geymonat's "ingenuous realism" (1987) that Geymonat himself regards as critically bankrupt. So Peckham concludes: "The writer, then, constructs a system of verbal signs to which the reader can respond in a variety of ways" (1970, 108). In sum, realism is a question more closely related to the reception rather than the creation of the text, as is the case with so many other issues—e.g., the pathetic, the sublime, the ironic— that fall within the horizon of the literary work. As such, it can clearly be accounted for through a phenomenology and pragmatics of literature. Marshall Brown, in a study of Hegelian inspiration (1981, 232), suggests the same approach when arguing that the term "realism" does not describe something to be found exclusively in the literary work, but, above all, in its effect on the readers: "Works are not intrinsically realistic; rather, they are realistic insofar as we concentrate in those silhouetings that create the effect of reality."

In the present book I have equally emphasized these reality effects because I do not believe in a pure theory of literary response without prior stimuli built into the text. Nowadays, the only approach that seems inappropriate for understanding realism is perhaps the genetic one, since phenomenology also posits the immanence of the text as a necessary factor in literary interpretation. This does not mean, as Fernando Lázaro Carreter cautions us in his classic study, to which I have often returned, that there exists a realist language, or even less, a "realist reality." What does exist is an intentional realist reader or reading.

BIBLIOGRAPHICAL REFERENCES

Abad Nebot, Francisco
1980 *Estudios filológicos*, University of Valladolid.

Abrams, M. H.
1953 *The Mirror and the Lamp. Romantic Theory and the Critical Tradition*, New York: Norton & Co.
1989 *Doing Things with Texts*, edited by Michael Fischer, New York and London: W. W. Norton & Co.

Adams, Jon-K.
1985 *Pragmatics and Fiction*, Amsterdam and Philadelphia: John Benjamins Publishing Co.

Agosti, Héctor P.
1945 *Defensa del realismo*, Montevideo: Editorial Pueblos Unidos.

Alas, Leopoldo
1882 "Del naturalismo," in Sergio Beser (editor), *Leopoldo Alas: Teoría y crítica de la novela española*, Barcelona: Laia, pp. 109–149.

Albaladejo Mayordomo, Tomás
1986 *Teoría de los mundos posibles y macroestructura narrativa*, University of Alicante.
1992 *Semántica de la narración: la ficción realista*, Madrid: Taurus.

Alpers, Paul
1983 "Convening and Convention in Pastoral Poetry," *New Literary History* XIV, 2, pp. 277–304.

Alpers, Svetlana
1976 "Describe or Narrate? A Problem in Realistic Representation," *New Literary History* VIII, 1, pp. 15–41.

Anderegg, Johanes
1973 *Fiktion und Kommunikation; ein Beitrag zur Theorie der Prosa*, Göttingen: Vendenhoek und Ruprecht.

Aristotle
1907 *On the Art of Poetry*, trans. and ed. by S. H. Butcher, 4th ed., London: MacMillan.
1980 *La poétique*. Text, translation, and notes by Roselyne Dupont-Roc and Jean Lallot, preface by Tzvetan Todorov, Paris: Seuil.

Arnheim, Rudolf
1980 "The Reach of Reality in the Arts," *Dipositio* V, 13–14, pp. 97–106.

Auerbach, Erich
1946 *Mimesis. Dargestellte Wirklichkeit in der abendländischen Literatur*, Bern: A. Francke AG Verlag. English edition: *Mimesis: The Representation of Reality in Western Literature*, trans. by Willard R. Trask, Princeton: Princeton University Press, 1953.
1953 "Epilegomena zu Mimesis," *Romanische Forschungen* 65, 1–2, pp. 1–18.

Baker, John Ross
1977 "From Imitation to Rhetoric: The Chicago Critics, Wayne C. Booth and *Tom Jones*," in Mark Spilka (editor), *Towards a Poetics of Fiction*, Bloomington: Indiana University Press, pp. 136–156.

Bakhtin, Mikhail
1989 *Teoría y estética de la novela*, Spanish translation by H. S. Kriukova and Vicente Cazcarra, Madrid: Taurus. (Original Russian edition, Moscow, 1975).

Bal, Mieke
1982 "Mimesis and Genre Theory in Aristotle's *Poetics*," *Poetics Today* 3, 1, pp. 171–180.
1984 "The Rhetoric of Subjectivity," *Poetics Today* 5, 2, pp. 337–376.

Barthes, Roland
1968 "L'effet de réel," *Communications* 11, pp. 84–89.
1970 *S/Z. Essais*, Paris: Seuil.

Barthes, Roland, and others
1968 "Le vraisemblable," *Communications* 11.
1982 *Littérature et réalité*, Paris: Seuil.

Bates, Elizabeth
1976 *Language and Context. The Acquisition of Pragmatics*, New York and San Francisco: Academic Press.

Beaugrande, Robert De
1981 "Design Criteria for Process Models of Reading," *Reading Research Quarterly* 16, pp. 261–315.

Becker, George J. (editor)
1963 *Documents of Modern Literary Realism*, Princeton: Princeton University Press.

Belevan, Harry
1976 *Teoría de lo fantástico. Apuntes para una dinámica de la literatura de expresión fantástica*, Barcelona: Anagrama.

Benet, Vicente J., and Bruguera, Maria Luisa (editors)
1994 *Ficcionalidad y escritura*, Castellón, Jaume I University.

Ben-Porat, Ziva
1986 "Represented Reality Models. European Autumn on Israeli Soil," *Poetics Today* 7, 1, pp. 29–58.

Benveniste, Emile
1966 "Nature du signe linguistique," in *Problèmes de linguistique générale* I, Paris: Gallimard, pp. 49–55.

Berger, Morroe
1977 *Real and Imagined Worlds. The Novel and the Social Science*, Cambridge: Harvard University Press.

Berger, Peter, and Luckmann, Thomas
1973 *The Social Construction of Reality. A Treatise in the Sociology of Knowledge*, Harmondsworth: Penguin Books.

Bersani, Leo
1982 "Le réalisme et la peur du désir," in Roland Barthes and others, pp. 47–80.

Bessière, Jean (editor)
1989 *Roman, réalités, réalismes*, Paris: P. U. F.

Bettetini, Gianfranco
1971 *L'indice del realismo*, Milano: Bompiani.

Bhaskar, Roy
1989 *Reclaiming Reality. A Critical Introduction to Contemporary Philosophy*, London and New York: Verso.

Black, Joel D.
1983 "The Literature of Play and the Literature of Power," *Poetics Today* 4, 4, pp. 773–782.

Bleich, David
1969 "Emotional Origins of Literary Meaning," *College of English* 31, 1, pp. 30–40.

Bobes Naves, María Del Carmen
1985 *Teoría general de la novela. Semiología de La Regenta*, Madrid.
1985b "*La Regenta* desde la estética de la recepción," *Letras de Deusto* 32, 7–24.

Booth, Wayne C.
1961 *The Rhetoric of Fiction*, Chicago and London: The University of Chicago Press.

Borgerhoff, E. B. O.
1938 "*Réalisme* and Kindred Words: Their Use as Terms of Literary Criticism in the First Half of the Nineteenth Century," *PMLA* 53, pp. 837–843.

Bornecque, J. H., and Cogny, P.
1963 *Réalisme et naturalisme: L' histoire, la doctrine, les oeuvres*, Paris: Hachette.

Bousoño, Carlos
1962 *Teoría de la expresión poética. Hacia una explicación del fenómeno lírico a través de textos españoles*, 5th edition, 2 vols., Madrid: Gredos, 1970.

Bowron, Bernard R.
1951 "Realism in America," *Comparative Literature* III, 3, pp. 268–285.

Boyd, John D.
1968 *The Function of Mimesis and its Decline*, Cambridge: Harvard University Press. (2nd edition, New York: Fordham University Press, 1980).

Boyer, Robert D. (editor)
1979 *Realism in European Theatre and Drama. 1870–1920. A Bibliography*, Wesport-London: Greenwood Press.

Boyle, Nicholas, and Swales, Martin (editors)
1986 *Realism in European Literature. Essays in Honor of J. P. Stern*, Cambridge: Cambridge University Press.

Bozal, Valeriano
1987 *Mimesis: las imágenes y las cosas*, Madrid: Visor.

Bradley, Raymond, and Swartz, Norman
1979 *Possible Worlds. An Introduction to Logic and its Philosophy*, Oxford: Basil Blackwell.

Brand, Gerd
1975 *Die grundlegenden Texte von Ludwig Wittgenstein*, Frankfurt am Main: Suhrkamp Verlag.

Brecht, Bertolt
1967 *Schriften zur Literatur und Kunst*, Frankfurt am Main: Suhrkamp Verlag. Selected by Werner Hecht.

Brinker, Menachem
1983 "Verisimilitude, Conventions and Beliefs," *New Literary History* XIV, 2, pp. 253–267.
1983b "On Realism's Relativism: A Reply to Nelson Goodman," *New Literary History* XIV, 2, pp. 273–276.

Brinkmann, Richard
1957 *Wirklichkeit und Illusion: Studien über Gehalt und Grenzen des Begriffs Realismus für die erzählende Dichtung des neuzehnten Jahrhunderts*, Tübingen: Niemeyer, 2nd edition 1966.

Brinkmann, Richard (editor)
1969 *Begriffsbestimmung des literarischen Realismus*, Darmstad: Wissenschaftliche Buchgessellschaft.

Brooke-Rose, Christine
1981 *A Rhetoric of the Unreal. Studies in Narrative and Structures, Specially of the Fantastic*, Cambridge: Cambridge University Press, 2nd edition, 1983.

Brooks, Peter
1983 "Fiction and its Referents: A Reappraisal," *Poetics Today* 4, 1, pp. 73–75.

Brown, Marshall
1961 "The Logic of Realism: A Hegelian Approach," *PMLA* 96, pp. 224–241.

Bruck, Jan
1982 "From Aristotelian Mimesis to "Bourgeois" Realism," *Poetics* II, pp 189–202.

Bruner, Jerome
1986 *Actual Minds, Possible Worlds*, Cambridge and London: Harvard University Press.

Brushwood, John S.
1981 "Sobre el referente y la transformación narrativa," *Semiosis* 6, pp 39–55.

Bruss, Elizabeth W.
1977 "The Game of Literature and Some Literary Games," *New Literary History* IX, 1, pp 153–172.

Bunge, Mario
1985 *Racionalidad y realismo*, Madrid: Alianza Editorial.

Camps, Victoria
1976 *Pragmática del lenguaje y filosofía analítica*, Barcelona: Península.

Castañeda, Héctor-Neri
1979 "Fiction and Reality: Their Fundamental Connections," *Poetics* 8, 1/2, pp 31–62.

Castilla Del Pino, Carlos (editor)
1988 *El discurso de la mentira*, Madrid: Alianza Editorial.
1989 *Teoría del personaje*, Madrid: Alianza Editorial.

Caudwell, Christopher
1937 *Illusion and Reality. A Study of the Sources of Poetry*, London: Lawrense & Wishart, 2nd edition 1977.

Chanady, Anaryll Beatrice
1985 *Magical Realism and the Fantastic. Resolved Versus Unresolved Antinomy*, New York and London: Garland Pub. Inc.

Charaudeau, P.
1983 *Langage et discours. Eléments de sémiolinguistique (Thèorie et pratique)*, Paris: Hachette.

Chateaux, Dominique
1976 "La sémantique du récit," *Semiotica* 18, pp 201–216.

Chiampi, Irlemar
1980 *O Realismo maravilhoso*, São Paulo: Perspectiva.

Chiari, Joseph
1960 *Realism and Imagination*, London: Barrie & Rockliff.

Chiarini, Paolo
1961 *L'avvanguardia e la poetica del realismo*, Bari: Laterza.

Cohn-Sherbok, Dan, and Irwin, Michael (editors)
1987 *Exploring Reality*, London: Allen & Unwin.

Combe, Dominique
1985 "Poésie, fiction, iconicité," *Poétique* 61, pp. 35–48.

Company-Ramón, Juan Miguel
1986 *La realidad como sospecha*, preface by Jenaro Taléns, Valencia
 and Minneapolis: Eutopías/Literatura.

Cooper, Charles R.
1976 "Empirical Studies of Response to Literature: Review and
 Suggestions," *Journal of Aesthetic Education* 3/4, pp. 77–93.

Crossman, Inge
1983 "Reference and the Reader," *Poetics Today* 4, 1, pp. 89–97.

Dahlhaus, Carl
1987 *Il realismo musicale: Per una storia della musica ottocen-
 tesca*, Bologna: Il Mulino.

Daix, Pierre
1968 *Nouvelle critique et art moderne*, Paris: Seuil.

Danon-Boileau, Laurent
1982 *Produire le fictif*, Paris: Klincksieck.

Davis, Robert Gorham
1951 "The Sense of the Real in English Fiction," *Comparative
 Literature* 111, 3, pp. 200–217.

De Man, Paul
1983 "Dialogue and Dialogism," *Poetics Today* 4, 1, pp. 99–107.

Derrida, Jacques
1967 *La voix et le phénomène. Introduction au problème du signe
 dans la phénoménologie de Husserl*, Paris: P. U. F.
1978 *La vérité en peinture*, Paris: Flammarion.

Derrida, Jacques and others
1975 *Mimesis/Des articulations*, Paris: Aubier Flammarion.

Dijk, Teun A. van (editor)
1976 *Pragmatics of Language and Literature*, Amsterdam: North-
 Holland.

Dijk, Teun, A. van
1980 *Texto y contexto (Semántica y pragmática del discurso)*, trans. by Juan Domingo Moyano, introduction by Antonio García Berrio. Madrid: Cátedra.
1981 *Studies in the Pragmatics of Discourse*, The Hague, Paris and New York: Mouton Publishers.

Doležel, Lubomir
1979 "Extensional and Intensional Narrative Worlds," *Poetics Today* 88, pp. 193–211.
1980 "Truth and Authenticity in Narrative," *Poetics Today* 1, 3, pp. 7–25.
1985 "La construction de mondes fictionnels à la Kafka," *Littérature* 57, pp. 80–92.
1988 "Mimesis and Possible Worlds," *Poetics Today* 9, 3, pp. 475–496.
1990 "Fictional Reference: Mimesis and Possible Worlds," in Mario J. Valdés (editor), *Toward a Theory of Comparative Literature*, New York: Peter Lang, pp. 109–124.

Doubrovsky, Serge
1971 "Littérature: Générativité de la phrase," in Various Authors, *Problèmes de l'analyse textuelle*, Montréal, Paris and Bruxelles: Didier, pp. 155–164.

Dubois, Jacques
1969 "Enoncé et énonciation," *Languages* 13, pp. 100–110.
1973 "Surcodage et protocole de lecture dans le roman naturaliste," *Poétique* 16, pp. 491–498.

Ducrot, Oswald, and Todorov, Tzvetan
1972 *Dictionnaire encyclopédique des sciences du langage*, Paris: Seuil.

Duchet, C.
1973 "Une écriture de la socialité," *Poétique* 16, pp. 446–454.

Durand, Gilbert
1960 *Les structures anthropologiques de l'imaginaire*, Paris: Bordas, 2nd edition 1969.
1961 *Le décor mytique de "La chartreuse de Parme." Les structures figuratives du roman stendhalien*, Paris: José Corti, 3rd edition 1983.
1964 *L'imagination symbolique*, Paris: P. U. F., 4th edition 1984.

Eagleton, Terry
1980 "Text, Ideology, Realism," in Edward W. Said (editor), *Literature and Society*, Baltimore and London: The Johns Hopkins University Press.

Eco, Umberto
1975 *Trattato di semiotica generale*, Milano: Bompiani.
1979 *Lector in fabula. La cooperazione interpretativa nei testi narrativi*, Milano: Bompiani.
1994 *Six Walks in the Fictional Woods*, Cambridge and London: Harvard University Press.

Ermarth, Elizabeth
1981 "Realism, Perspective, and the Novel," *Critical Inquiry* 7, 3, pp. 499–520.

Even-Zohar, Itamar
1985 "Les règles d'insertion des 'réalèmes' dans la narration," *Littérature* 57, pp. 109–118.

Fanger, Donald
1967 *Dostoievsky and Romantic Realism*, Cambridge and London: Harvard University Press.

Fellmann, Ferdinand
1982 *Fenomenología y expresionismo*, trans. by Enrique Müller del Castillo, Barcelona and Caracas: Alfa.

Feyerabend, P. K.
1981 *Realism, Rationalism and Scientific Method. Philosophical Papers*. Vol. 1, Cambridge: Cambridge University Press.

Fischer, Ernst
1967 *La necesidad del arte*, trans. by J. Solé-Tura, Barcelona: Península, 5th edition 1978.
1972 *El artista y su época*, trans. by María Nolla, Madrid: Fundamentos.

Fish, Stanley E.
1975 "Facts and Fictions: A Reply to Ralph Rader," *Critical Inquiry* 1, 4, pp. 883–891.
1976 "Interpreting the Variorum," *Critical Inquiry* 2, 3, pp. 465–485.
1980 *Is There a Text in this Class?: The Authority of Interpretative Communities*, Cambridge: Harvard University Press.

Flaubert, Gustave
1973 *Correspondence. I (janvier 1830 à juin 1851)*, ed. by Jean Bruneau, Paris: Gallimard.
1980 *Correspondence. II (juillet 1851 à decembre 1858)*, ed. by Jean Bruneau, Paris: Gallimard.

Forest, H. U.
1926 " 'Réalisme,' journal de Duranty," *Modern Philology* 24, pp. 463–479.

Fox, Ralph
1975 *La novela y el pueblo*, trans. by Vicente Romano García, Madrid: Akal Editor.

Freedman, Ralph
1976 "Intentionality and the Literary Object," *Contemporary Literature*. Also in Murray Krieger and L. S. Dembo, *Directions for Criticism: Structuralism and Its Alternatives*, Madison: University of Wisconsin Press, 1977, pp. 137–159.

Frege, Gottlob
1892 "Über Sinn und Bedeutung," *Zeitschrift für Philosophie und philosophische Kritik*, NF 100 (1892), pp. 25–50.

Frye, Northrop
1971 *The Critical Path. An Essay on the Social Context of Literary Criticism*, Bloomington: Indiana University Press.
1976 "The Responsibilities of the Critic," *MLN*, pp. 797–813.

Furst, Lilian R. (editor)
1992 *Realism*, London and New York: Longman.

Fuster, J.
1957 *El descrédito de la realidad*, Barcelona: Seix Barral.

Gabriel, Gottfried
1975 *Fiktion und Wahrheit: Eine semantische Theorie der Literatur*, Stuttgart: Fromman Verlag.
1979 "Fiction. A Semantic Approach," *Poetics* 8, pp. 245–255.

Gadamer, Hans-Georg
1965 *Warhheit und Methode*, Tübingen: J. C. B. Mohr. English edition: *Truth and Method*, New York: Continuum, 1975.
1982 *L'Art de comprendre. Herméneutique et tradition philosophique*, trans. by Marianna Simon, Paris: Aubier-Montaigne.

Gaillard, Françoise
1984 "The Great Illusion of Realism, or the Real as Representation,"
    Poetics Today 5, 4, pp. 753–766.

Garaudy, R.
1964 *Hacia un realismo sin fronteras*, Buenos Aires: Lautaro.

García Berrio, Antonio
1977 *Formación de la teoría literaria moderna. La tópica horaciana
    en Europa*, Madrid: Cupsa.
1979 "Lingüística, Literalidad/Poeticidad (Gramática, Pragmática,
    Texto)," 1616, 2, pp. 125–170.
1985 *La construcción imaginaria en "Cántico" de Jorge Guillén*,
    Limoges: Université de Limoges.

García Berrio, Antonio, and Hernández Fernández, Teresa
1988 *"Ut poesis pictura." Poética del arte visual*, Madrid: Tecnos.

Gasparov, Boris
1978 "The Narrative Text as an Act of Communication," *New
    Literary History* IX, 2, pp. 245–261.

Gass, William H.
1958 *Fiction and the Figures of Life*, New York: Knopf.

Genette, Gérard
1968 "Vraisemblance et motivation," *Communications* 11, pp. 5–21.
1972 *Figures III*, Paris: Seuil.
1987 *Seuils*, Paris: Seuil.
1991 *Fiction et diction*, Paris: Seuil.

Genot, Gérard
1968 "L'écriture libératrice. Le vraisemblable dans la *Jerusalem
    delivrée* du Tasse," *Communications* 11, pp. 34–58.

Geymonat, Ludovico
1977 *Scienza e realismo*, Milano: Feltrinelli.

Gilbert, Margaret
1983 "Notes on the Concept of a Social Convention," *New Literary
    History* XIV, 2, pp. 225–251.

Girard, René
1978 *"To Double Business Bound": Essays on Literature, Mimesis
    and Anthropology*, Baltimore and London: The Johns Hopkins
    University Press.

Goldman, Lucien
1964 *Pour une sociologie du roman*, Paris: Gallimard.

Gombrich, Ernst H.
1959 *Art and Illusion. A Study in the Psychology of Pictorial Representation*, Oxford: Phaidon Press Ltd.
1982 *The Image and the Eye: Further Studies in the Psychology of Pictorial Representation*, Ithaca: Cornell University Press.
1984 "Representation and Misrepresentation," *Critical Inquiry* 11, pp. 195–201.

Gombrich, E. H., Hochbert, J., and Black, M.
1972 *Art, Perception and Reality*, Baltimore and London: The John Hopkins University Press.

Goodman, Nelson
1968 *The Languages of Art*, Indianapolis, New York and Kansas City: Bobbs-Merrill.
1981 "Routes of Reference," *Critical Inquiry* 8, pp. 121–132.
1983 "Realism, Relativism, and Reality," *New Literary History* XIV, 2, pp. 269–272.

Grant, Damian
1970 *Realism*, London: Methuen & Co., 2nd edition 1978.

Gray, Bennison
1975 *The Phenomenon of Literature*, The Hague and Paris: Mouton.

Greenwood, E. E.
1962 "Reflections on Professor Wellek's Concept of Realism," *Neophilologus* XLVI, 2, pp. 89–97.

Grice, H. P.
1969 "Meaning," in T. M. Olshewsky (editor), *Problems in the Philosophy of Language*, New York: Holt, Rinehart & Winston, pp.251–259.
1975 "Logic and Conversation," in P. Cole and J. L. Morgan (editors), *Syntax and Semantics, 3: Speech Acts*, New York and London: Academic Press, pp. 41–58.

Grivel, Charles
1973 *Production de l'intérêt romanesque. Un état du texte (1870–1880), un essai de constitution de sa théorie*, The Hague and Paris: Mouton.

1973b *Production de l'intérêt romanesque. Un état du texte (1870–1880), un essai de constitution de sa théorie (volume complémentaire)*, Amstelveen: Hoekstra Offset.

Groeben, Norbert
1981 "The Empirical Study of Literature and Literary Evaluation," *Poetics* 10, pp. 381–394.

Gullón, Germán
1983 *La novela como acto imaginativo*, Madrid: Taurus.

Hagen, Margaret A.
1986 *Varieties of Realism. Geometries of Representational Art*, Cambridge: Cambridge University Press.

Hamburger, Käte
1957 *Die Logik der Dichtung*, Stuttgart: Ernst Klett Verlag; 2nd edition 1968. English edition: *The Logic of Literature*, trans. by M. J. Rose, Bloomington and London: Indiana University Press, 1973.
1979 *Wahrheit und ästhetische Wahrheit*, Stuttgart: Klett-Cotta.

Hamon, Philippe
1972 "Qu'est-ce qu'une description?" *Poétique* 12, pp. 465–487.
1973 "Un discours contraint," *Poétique* 16, pp. 411–445.
1980 "L'énoncé descriptif et sa construction thèorique," *Dispositio* V, 13–14, pp. 55–95.
1981 *Introduction à l'analyse du descriptif*, Paris: Hachette.
1985 "Thème et effet de réel," *Poétique* 64, pp. 495–503.

Hancher, Michael
1972 "Three Kinds of Intention," *MLN* 87, 7, pp. 827–851.

Harding, D. W.
1962 "Psychological Process in the Reading of Fiction," *British Journal of Aesthetics* 2, pp. 133–147.

Harshaw (Hrushovski), Benjamin
1984 "Fictionality and Fields of Reference. Remarks on a Theoretical Framework," *Poetics Today* 5, 2, pp. 227–251.
1985 "Présentation et représentation dans la fiction littéraire," *Littérature* 57, pp. 6–30.

Hartman, Geoffrey H.
1975 *The Fate of Reading and other Essays*, Chicago and London: University of Chicago Press.

Hatfield, Henry C.
1951 "Realism in the German Novel," *Comparative Literature* 111, 3, pp. 234–252.

Hauptmeier, Helmut, and Viehoff, Reinhold
1983 " Empirical Research on the Basis of Bio-Epistemology. A New Paradigm for the Study of Literature," *Poetics Today* 4, 1, pp. 153–171.

Hegel, G. W. F.
1807 *The Phenomenology of Mind*, trans. by J. B. Baillie, London: G. Allen and Unwin, 1931.

Heintz, John
1979 "Reference and Inference in Fiction," *Poetics* 8, pp. 85–99.

Heller, Erich
1955 "The Realistic Fallacy: A Discussion of Realism in Literature," *Listener* 53, pp. 888–889.

Hemmings, F. W. J. (editor)
1974 *The Age of Realism*, Harmondsworth: Penguin/Pelican Books.

Henrich, D., and Iser, W. (editors)
1983 *Funktionen des Fiktiven*, Munich: Fink.

Hirsch, E. D.
1967 *Validity in Interpretation*, New Haven: Yale University Press.
1976 *The Aims of Interpretation*, Chicago and London: The University of Chicago Press.
1983 "Beyond Convention?" *New Literary History* XIV, 2, pp. 389–397.
1984 "Meaning and Significance Reinterpreted," *Critical Inquiry* 11, pp. 202–225.

Hoek, Leo H.
1980 *La marque du titre. Dispositifs sémiotiques d'une pratique textuelle*, The Hague: Mouton.

Holland, Norman
1968 *The Dynamics of Literary Response*, New York: Oxford University Press.
1973 *Poems in Persons: An Introduction to the Psychoanalysis of Literature*, New York: Norton.
1975 *5 Readers Reading*, New Haven and London: Yale University Press.

Hollowell, John
1977 *Fact and Fiction. The New Journalism and the Nonfiction Novel*, Chapel Hill: The University of North Carolina Press.

Hospers, John
1964 *Meaning and Truth in Art*, Hamden: Archon Books.

Howell, Robert
1979 "Fictional Objects: How They Are and How They Aren't," *Poetics* 8, pp. 129–177.

Hristič, Jovan
1977 "The Problem of Realism in Modern Drama," *New Literary History* VII, 2, pp. 311–318.

Hume, Kathryn
1984 *Fantasy and Mimesis. Responses to Reality in Western Literature*, London: Methuen.

Husserl, Edmund
1913 *Ideen zu einer reinen Phänomenologie und phänomenologischen Philosophie*, Halle: Max Niemeyer.
1929 *Logische Untersuchungen*, Hamburg: Max Niemeyer Verlag.
1973 *Die Idee der Phänomenologie. Fünf Vorlesungen*, The Hague: Martinus Nijhoff.

Ihwe, Jens F., and Rieser, Hannes
1979 "Normative and Descriptive Theory of Fiction. Some Contemporary Issues," *Poetics* 8, 1/2, pp. 63–84.

Imbert, Patrick
1983 "La structure de la description réaliste dans la littérature européenne," *Semiotica* 44, 1/2, pp. 95–122.

Ingarden, Roman
1931 *Das literarische Kunstwerk*, Tübingen: Max Niemeyer Verlag, 3rd edition 1965.
1962 "A Marginal Commentary on Aristotle's *Poetics* (I & 11)," *Journal of Aesthetics and Art Criticism* 20, 2 and 3, pp. 163–173 and 273–285.
1968 *Vom Erkennen des literarischen Kunstwerks*, Darmstadt: Wissenschaftliche Buchgesellschaft. English edition: *The Cognition of the Literary Work of Art*, trans. by Ruth Ann Crowley and Kenneth R. Olson, Evanston: Northwestern University Press.

Iser, Wolfgang
1972 *Der implizite Leser: Kommunikationsformen des Romans von Bunyan bis Beckett*, Munich: Wilhelm Fink. English edition: *The Implied Reader. Patterns of Communication in Prose Fiction from Bunyan to Beckett*, Baltimore and London: The Johns Hopkins University Press, 1974.
1975 "Die Wirklichkeit der Fiktion," in Rainer Warning (editor), *Rezeptionsästhetik. Theorie und Praxis*, Munich: UTB, pp. 277–324.
1975b "The Indeterminacy of the Text: A Critical Reply," in Elinor Schaffer (editor), *Comparative Criticism. A Yearbook*, 2, Cambridge: Cambridge University Press, pp. 27–47.
1976 *Der Akt des Lesens: Theorie ästhetischer Wirkung*, Munich: Fink. English edition: *The Act of Reading: A Theory of Aesthetic Response*, Baltimore: The Johns Hopkins University Press, 1978.
1983 "Akte des Fingierens, oder: Was ist das Fiktive im fiktionalen Text?" in D. Henrich and W. Iser (editors).
1993 *The Fictive and the Imaginary*, Baltimore and London: The Johns Hopkins University Press.

Jacquot, Jean (editor)
1960 *Réalisme et poésie au thèatre*, Paris: C. N. R. S., 2nd edition 1967.

Jakobson, Roman
1921 "Du réalisme artistique," in Tzvetan Todorov (editor), *Théorie de la littérature*, Paris: Seuil, 965, pp. 98–108.
1971 "Quest for Essence of Language," in *Selected Writings* 11, *Word and Language*, The Hague and Paris: Mouton, pp. 345–359.

James, Henry
1884 "The Art of Fiction," in *Literary Criticism: Essays on Literature; American Writers; English Writers*, New York: The Library of America, 1984.

Jauss, Hans Robert
1977 *Ästhetische Erfahrung und literarische Hermeneutik*, Munich: Wilhelm Fink.
1979 "La jouissance esthétique. Les expériences fondamentales de la poiesis, de l'aisthesis et de la catharsis," *Poétique* 39, pp. 261–274.
1985 "La perfection, fascination de l'imaginaire," *Poétique* 61, pp. 3–21.

Juhl, P. D.
1980 *Interpretation. An Essay in the Philosophy of Literary Criticism*, Princeton: Princeton University Press.

Kahn, Scholom J.
1952–5 "What does a Critic Analyze? On a Phenomenological Approach to Literature," *Philosophy and Phenomenological Research* VIII, pp. 237–245.

Kaplan, Amy
1988 *The Social Construction of American Realism*, Chicago and London: The University of Chicago Press.

Kaufmann, Walter
1966 "Literature and Reality," in Sidney Hook (editor), *Art and Philosophy: A Symposium*, New York: New York University Press, pp. 250–340.

Kennard, Jean E.
1981 "Convention Coverage or How to Read Your Own Life," *New Literary History* XIII, 1, pp. 69–88.

Kermode, Frank
1966 *The Sense of an Ending. Studies in the Theory of Fiction*, London, Oxford, New York: Oxford University Press.
1983 "Institutional Control of Interpretation," *Essays on Fiction 1971–1982*, London: Melbourne & Henley, Routledge & Kegan Paul, pp. 168–184.

Kindt, W.
1981 "Some Foundational and Methodical Problems of the Empirical Theory of Literature," *Poetics* 10, pp. 483–513.

Klementz-Belgardt, Edith
1981 "American Research on Response to Literature: The Empirical Studies," *Poetics* 10, pp. 357–380.

Kochler, Hans
1986 *Phenomenological Realism: Selected Essays*, Frankfurt am Main and New York: Peter Lang.

Koelb, Clayton
1984 *The Incredulous Reader. Literature and the Function of Disbelief*, Ithaca and London: Cornell University Press.

Kohl, Stephan
1977 *Realismus: Theorie und Geschichte*, Munich: Fink/UTB.

Koller, Hermann
1954 *Die Mimesis in der Antike: Nachahmung, Darstellung, Ausdruck*, Berne: Francke.

Köpeczi, Béla, and Juhász, Péter (editors)
1966 *Littérature et réalité*, Budapest: Akademiai Kiado.

Krieger, Murray
1974 "Fiction, History, and Empirical Reality," *Critical Inquiry* 1, 2, pp. 335–360.
1984 "The Ambiguities of Representation and Illusion: An E. H. Gombrich Retrospective," *Critical Inquiry* 11, pp. 181–194.

Kristeva, Julia
1968 "La productivité dite texte," *Communications* 11, pp. 59–83.

Kristeva, Julia, and others
1975 *La traversée des signes*, Paris: Seuil.

Kronik, John W.
1988 "La danza de las basuras: La poética de la descripción y el arte realista," *Insula* 502, pp. 1–2.

Kuroda, S. Y.
1976 "Reflections on the Foundations of Narrative Theory from a Linguistic Point of View," in Teun A. van Dijk (editor), *Pragmatics of Language*, pp. 107–140.

La Matina, Marcello
1985 "Realismo e indicalitá nei testi narrativi," *Versus* 42, pp. 75–84.

Lafargue, Claude
1983 *La valeur littéraire. Figuration et usages sociaux des fictions*, Paris: Fayard.

Landwehr, Jürgen
1975 *Text und Fiktion*, Munich: Fink.

Lattre, Alain De
1975 *Le réalisme selon Zola. Archéologie d'une intelligence*, Paris: P. U. F.

Lausberg, Heinrich
1960 *Handbuch der literarischen Rhetorik. Eine Grundlegung der Literaturwissenschaft*, Munich: Max Heuber Verlag.

Lavis, Georges
1971 "Le texte littéraire, le référent, le réel, le vrai," *Cahiers d'analyse textuelle* 13, pp. 7–22.

Lázaro Carreter, Fernando
1969 "El realismo como concepto crítico literario," *Cuadernos Hispanoamericanos*, 238–240, pp. 128–151. Also in *Estudios de poética*, Madrid: Taurus, 1976, pp. 121–142.
1970 "Breves puntualizaciones sobre el artículo de Sr. Rey Álvarez," *Cuadernos Hispanoamericanos* pp. 248–249.
1980 *Estudios de lingüística*, Barcelona: Crítica.

Leclaire, S.
1971 "Le réel dans le texte," *Littérature* 3, pp. 30–32.

Leibniz, Gottfried Wilhelm
1875 *Die Philosophischen Schriften*, ed. C. J. Gerhard, v. I–VIII, Berlin.

Lessing, G. Ephraim
1766 *Laokoon oder über die Grenzen der Malerei und Poesie.* English edition: *Laocoon. An Essay on the Limits of Painting and Poetry*, trans. with introduction and notes by Edward Allen McCormick, Baltimore: The Johns Hopkins University Press, 1984.

Levin, Harry
1951 "What Is Realism?" *Comparative Literature* III, 3, pp. 193–199.
1963 *The Gates of Horn (A Study of Five French Realists)*, New York: Oxford University Press.
1972 "On the Dissemination of Realism," in *Grounds for Comparisons*, Cambridge: Harvard University Press, pp. 244–261.

Levin, George (editor)
1993 *Realism and Representation. Essays on the Problem of Realism in Relation to Science, Literature, and Culture*, Madison: The University of Wisconsin Press.

Levine, Samuel R.
1976 "Concerning what Kind of Speech Act a Poem Is," in Teun A. van Dijk (editor), *Pragmatics of Language*, pp. 141–160.

Lewis, C. S.
1961 *An Experiment in Criticism*, Cambridge: Cambridge University Press.

Lewis, Thomas E.
1979 "Notes Towards a Theory of the Referent," *PMLA* 94, 3, pp. 459–475.
1985 "El acto referencial," *Eutopías* 1, 3, pp. 177–201.

Likhachov, Dimitri S.
1986 "Sobre el realismo y su definición," ed. and trans. by Desiderio Navarro, *Textos y Contextos. Una ojeada en la teoría literaria mundial*, La Habana: Arte y Literatura.

Lobsien, Eckhard
1975 *Theorie literarischer Illusionsbildung*, Stuttgart: Metzler.

López, Ignacio Javier
1989 *Realismo y ficción. "La Desheredada" de Benito Pérez Galdós*, Barcelona: PPU.

López Grigera, Luisa
1986 "Sobre el realismo literario del Siglo de Oro," in *Actas del VIII Congreso de la Asociación Internacional de Hispanistas*, Madrid: Istmo, pp. 201–209.

Lotman, Yuri M.
1973 *La structure du texte artistique*, trans. by A. Fournier, B. Kreise, A. Malleret and J. Young under the direction of H. Meschonnic. Paris: Gallimard. Spanish edition: *Estructura del texto artístico*, trans. by Victoriano Imbert, Madrid: Istmo, 1978.

Lovell, Terry
1980 *Pictures of Reality. Aesthetics, Politics and Pleasure*, London: British Phil. Institute.

Lukács, Georg
1955 *Probleme des Realismus*, Berlin/Spandau: Hermann Luchterhand Verlag.
1958 *Wider den missverstandenen Realismus*, Hamburg: Claasen.
1963 *Ästhetik. I. Teil. Die Eigenart des Ästhetischen*, Berlin/Spandau: Hermann Luchterhand Verlag.
1965 *Ensayos sobre el realismo*, trans. by J. J. Sebreli, Buenos Aires: Ediciones Siglo Veinte.
1977 *Materiales sobre el realismo*, trans. by Manuel Sacristán, Barcelona: Grijalbo.

Lukács, G., Adorno, T. W., Jakobson, R., Fischer, E., Barthes, R.
1969 *Polémica sobre realismo*, Buenos Aires: Tiempo Contemporáneo.

Lyons, J.
1981 *Language, Meaning and Context,* London William Collins & Sons.

Lyons, J. D., and Nichols, S. G. (editors)
1982 *Mimesis: From Mirror to Method, Augustine to Descartes,* Hanover and London: University Press of New England.

Lyotard, Jean-François
1974 *Discours, Figure,* Paris: Editions Klincksieck.

Maffesoli, M. (editor)
1980 *La galaxie de l'imaginaire. Dérive autour de l'oeuvre de G. Durand,* Paris: Berg International.

Mailloux, Steven
1983 "Convention and Context," *New Literary History* XIV, 2, pp. 399–407.

Martin, Richard M.
1958 *Truth and Denotation,* Chicago: The University of Chicago Press.

Martínez Bonati, Félix
1960 *La estructura de la obra literaria. Una investigación de filosofía del lenguaje y estética,* 3rd edition, Barcelona: Ariel
1978 "El acto de escribir ficciones," *Dispositio* III, 7–8, pp. 137–144.
1980 "Representation and Fiction," *Dispositio* V, 13–14, pp. 19–33.

Martino, Pierre
1913 *Le roman réaliste sous le Second Empire,* Geneva: Slaktine Reprints, 1972.

Maturana, Humberto R.
1970 *Biology of Cognition,* Urbana Biological Computer Laboratory, University of Illinois.
1980 *Erkennen: Die Organisation und Verkörperung von Wirklichkeit,* Braunschweig-Wiesbaden: Vieweg.

Maupassant, Guy
1888 *Pierre et Jean,* ed. by Pierre Cogny, Paris: Garnier, 1959.

Marx, Karl, and Engels, Friedrich
1954 *Sur la littérature et l'art,* Paris: Editions Sociales.

McDowall, Arthur
1918 *Realism: A Study in Art and Thought,* London: Constable & Co.

McKeon, Richard
1936 "Literary Criticism and the Concept of Imitation in Antiquity,"
    Modern Philology XXXIV, pp. 1–35. Also in R. S. Crane (editor),
    Critics and Criticism: Ancient and Modern, Chicago: The
    University of Chicago Press, 1952, pp. 147–175.

Mena, Lucila-Inés
1975 "Hacia una formulación teórica del realismo mágico," *Bulletin
    Hispanique* 77, 3–4, pp. 395–407.

Merleau-Ponty, Maurice
1945 *Phénoménologie de la perception*, Paris: Gallimard.

Mignolo, Walter D.
1982 "Sobre las condiciones de la ficción literaria," in *Textos, mod-
    elos y metáforas*, Xalapa: University of Vera Cruz, 1984, pp.
    223–240.

Miller, James E.
1976 "Henry James in Reality," *Critical Inquiry* 2, 3, pp. 585–604.

Miner, Earl
1976 "The Objective Fallacy," *PTL* 1, pp. 11–31.

Mitterand, Henri
1973 "Fonction narrative et fonction mimétique. Les personages de
    Germinal," *Poétique* 16, pp. 477–490.
1980 *Le discours du roman*, Paris: P. U. F.
1994 *L'illusion réaliste. De Balzac à Aragon*, Paris: P. U. F.

Morawski, Stefan
1963 "Le réalisme comme catégorie artistique," *Recherches inter-
    nationales à la lumière du marxisme* 388, pp. 52–75.
1974 *Inquiries into the Fundamentals of Aesthetics*, Cambridge:
    M. I. T. Press.

Morris, Charles W.
1985 *Symbolism and Reality. A Study in the Nature of Mind*, pref-
    ace by George H. Mead and introductory essay by Achim
    Eschbach, Amsterdam: John Benjamins Publ.

Moser, Walter
1984 "The Factual in Fiction. The Case of Robert Musil," *Poetics
    Today* 5, 2, pp. 411–428.

Mukařovsky, Jan
1936 "El arte como hecho semiológico," in *Escritos de estética y semiótica del arte*, ed. by Jordi Llovet, Barcelona, 1977, pp. 35–43.

Neefs, Jacques
1973 "La figuration réaliste. L' exemple de *Madame Bovary*," *Poétique* 16, pp. 466–476.

Nemoianu, Virgil
1984 "Societal Models as Substitute Reality in Literature," *Poetics Today* 5, 2, pp. 275–297.

Nochlin, Linda
1971 *Realism*, Harmondsworth: Penguin.

Nuttall, A. D.
1983 *A New Mimesis. Shakespeare and the Representation of Reality*, London: Methuen.

O'Connor, D. J.
1975 *The Correspondence Theory of Truth*, London: Hutchinson.

Odmark, John
1979 "Ingarden and the Concretization of the Literary Text," in *Proceedings of the IXth Congress of the International Comparative Literature Association*, 2, Innsbruck, pp. 223–226.

Ohmann, Richard
1971 "Speech Acts and the Definition of Literature," *Philosophy and Rhetoric* 4, pp. 1–19.

Oleza, Juan
1976 *Sincronía y diacronía. La dialéctica del discurso poético*, Valencia: Prometeo, pp. 15–60.

Olsen, Stein Haugom
1978 *The Structure of Literary Understanding*, Cambridge: Cambridge University Press.
1982 "The 'Meaning' of a Literary Work," *New Literary History* XIV, 1, pp. 13–32.

Orr, John
1977 *Tragic Realism and Modern Society. Studies in the Sociology of the Modern Novel*, London: MacMillan Press.

Pagnini, Marcello
1980 *Pragmatica della letteratura*, Palermo: Sellerio Editore.

Pascal, Roy
1977 "Narrative Fictions and Reality. A Comment on Frank Kermode's *The Sense of an Ending*," *Novel* 11, 1, pp. 40–50.

Pavel, Thomas G.
1976 "Possible Worlds in Literary Semantics," *The Journal of Aesthetics and Art Criticism* XXXIV, 2, pp. 165–176.
1979 "Fiction and the Casual Theory of Names," *Poetics* 88, pp. 179–191.
1983 "The Borders of Fiction," *Poetics Today* 4, 1, pp. 83–88.
1985 "Convention et représentation," *Littérature* 57, pp. 31–47.
1986 *Fictional Worlds*, Cambridge and London: Harvard University Press.

Peckham, Morse
1970 "Is the Problem of Literary Realism a Pseudoproblem?" *Critique. Studies in Modern Fiction* XII, pp. 95–112.

Petrosky, A. R.
1976 "The Effects of Reality Perception and Fantasy on Response to Literature: Two Case Studies," *Research in the Teaching of English*, 3, pp. 239–258.

Phillips, Terry
1971 "Poetry in the Junior School," *English in Education* 5, 3, pp. 51–62.

Plebe, Armando
1969 *Che cosa é l'estetica sovietica*, Roma: Astrolabio.

Poggioli, Renato
1951 "Realism in Russia," *Comparative Literature* III, 3, pp. 253–267.

Popper, Karl R.
1964 "Nota histórica sobre la verosimilitud (1964)," in *Conjeturas y refutaciones. El desarrollo del conocimiento científico*, Barcelona and Buenos Aires: Paidos, 1983, 3rd edition, pp. 475–478.
1968 "Algunas indicaciones adicionales sobre la verosimilitud," in *Conjeturas y refutaciones*, pp. 478–482. 1st English edition: *Conjectures and Refutations: The Growth of Scientific Knowledge*, New York and London: Basic Books, 1962.

Pozuelo Yvancos, José María
1993 *Poética de la ficción*, Madrid: Editorial Síntesis.

Pratt, Mary Louise
1977 *Toward a Speech Act Theory of Literary Discourse*, Bloomington: Indiana University Press.

Preisendanz, Wolfgang
1977 *Wege des Realismus*, Munich: Wilhelm Fink.

Prendergast, Christopher
1986 *The Order of Mimesis. Balzac, Stendhal, Nerval, Flaubert*, Cambridge: Cambridge University Press.

Price, Martin
1973 "The Fictional Contract," in F. Brady, J. Palmer, and M. Price, *Literary Theory and Structure*, New Haven and London: Yale University Press, pp. 151–178.

Pujante Sánchez, José David
1992 *Mimesis y siglo XX*, Murcia: University of Murcia.

Purves, Alan C.
1972 *Literature and the Reader: Research in Response to Literature, Reading Interests and the Teaching of Literature*, Urbana: National Council of Teachers of English.

Putnam, Hilary
1983 "Is There a Fact of the Matter about Fiction?," *Poetics Today* 4, 1, pp. 71–81.

Rabinowitz, Peter J.
1977 "Truth in Fiction. A Reexamination of Audiences," *Critical Inquiry* 4, 1, pp. 121–141.

Rader, Ralph
1974 "Fact, Theory, and Literary Explanation," *Critical Inquiry* 1, 2, pp. 245–272.

Raffa, Piero
1967 *Avanguardia e realismo*, Milano: Rizzoli.
1971 *Introducción a la estética*, trans. by Ricardo Mazo, Barcelona: Península.

Rasmussen, Dennis
1974 *Poetry and Truth*, The Hague and Paris: Mouton.

Redmond, James (editor)
1980 *Drama and Mimesis*, Cambridge: Cambridge University Press.

Reeve, Clara
1785 *The Progress of Romance and the History of Charoba, Queen of Aegypt*, New York: The Facsimile Text Society, 1930.

Reeves, Charles Eric
1986 "The Language of Convention. Literature and Consensus," *Poetics Today* 7, 1, pp. 3–28.

Reichert, John
1981 "Do Poets Ever Mean What They Say?," *New Literary History* 13, pp. 53–67.

Reis, Carlos
1987 *Para una semiótica de la ideología*, Madrid: Taurus. English edition: *Towards a Semiotics of Ideology*, Berlin and New York: Mouton and DeGruyter, 1993.

Reisz De Rivarola, Susana
1979 "Ficcionalidad, referencia, tipos de ficción literaria," *Lexis* 3, 2, pp. 99–170.

Rey Álvarez, Alfonso
1970 "En torno al realismo como concepto crítico-literario," *Cuadernos Hispanoamericanos*, 248–249, pp. 533–542.

Reyes, Alfonso
1942 *La experiencia literaria*, México: F. C. E., 3rd edition 1983.
1944 *El deslinde. Prolegómenos a la teoría literaria*, México: F. C. E., 3rd edition 1983.

Rico, Francisco
1988 *Problemas del "Lazarillo,"* Madrid: Cátedra.

Ricoeur, Paul
1969 *Le conflit des interprétations. Essais d'herméneutique*, Paris: Seuil.
1975 *La métaphore vive*, Paris: Seuil.
1981 "Mimesis and Representation," *Annals of Scholarship* II, 3, pp. 15–32.
1983 *Temps et récit. Tome I*, Paris: Seuil.
1984 *Temps et récit. Tome II. La configuration du temps dans le récit de fiction*, Paris: Seuil.
1985 *Temps et récit. Tome III. Le temps raconté*, Paris: Seuil.

Richards, I. A.
1929 *Practical Criticism*, London: Routledge and Kegan Paul.

Riffaterre, Michael
1966 "La descripción de las estructuras poéticas: Dos aproximaciones al poema de Baudelaire "Les Chats," in José Vidal Beneyto (editor), *Posibilidades y límites del análisis estructural*, Madrid: Editora Nacional, 1981, pp. 163–201.
1971 "L'explication des faits littéraires," in Various Authors, *L'enseignement de la littérature*, Paris: Plon.
1972 "Système d'un genre descriptif," *Poétique 9*, pp. 15–30.
1978 "The Referential Fallacy," *Columbia Review 57*, pp. 21–35.
1979 *La production du texte*, Paris: Seuil.
1982 "L'illusion référentielle," in Roland Barthes and others, pp. 91–118.
1984 "Intertextual Representation: On Mimesis as Interpretative Discourse," *Critical Inquiry 11*, pp. 141–162.
1990 *Fictional Truth*, Baltimore: The Johns Hopkins University Press.

Risco, Antonio
1982 *Literatura y fantasía*, Madrid: Taurus.
1982b *Literatura y figuración*, Madrid: Gredos.
1987 *Literatura fantástica de lengua española*, Madrid: Taurus.

Robbe-Grillet, Alain
1963 *Pour un noveau roman*, Paris: Minuit.

Robin, Régine
1986 *Le réalisme socialiste; Une esthétique impossible*, Paris: Payot. English edition: *Socialist Realism: An Impossible Aesthetic*, trans. by Catherine Porter, foreword by Leon Robel, Stanford: Stanford University Press, 1992.

Rorty, Richard
1975 "Realism and Reference," *The Monist 59*, pp. 321–340.

Rosenblat, Louise M.
1978 *The Reader, the Text, the Poem. The Transactional Theory of the Literary Work*, London and Amsterdam: Southern Illinois University Press/Feffer & Simmons.

Rosset, Clement
1977 *Le réel. Traité de l'idiotie*, Paris: Minuit.

Rossum-Guyon, Françoise Van
1970 *Critique du roman. Essai sur* La Modification *de Michel Butor*,
      Paris: Gallimard.

Routley, Richard
1979 "The Semantical Structure of Fictional Discourse," *Poetics* 8,
      pp. 3–30.

Ruffinato, Aldo
1989 *Sobre textos y mundos*, Murcia: University of Murcia.

Russell, Bertrand
1940 *An Inquiry into Meaning and Truth*, London: George Allen
      and Unwin Ltd.

Ruthrof, Horst
1981 *The Reader's Construction of Narrative*, London and Boston:
      Routledge & Kegan Paul.

Sager, Peter
1981 *Nuevas formas del realismo*, Madrid: Alianza Editorial.

Salinas, Pedro
1940 *Reality and the Poet in Spanish Poetry*, Baltimore: The Johns
      Hopkins University Press.

Salvan, Albert J.
1951 "L'essence du réalisme français," *Comparative Literature* III, 3,
      pp. 218–233.

Sandbank, Shimon
1985 "The Object-Poem. In Defence of Referentiality," *Poetics Today*
      6, 3, pp. 461–473.

San Martín, Javier
1986 *La estructura del método fenomenológico*, Madrid: Uned.
1987 *La fenomenología de Husserl como utopía de la razón*,
      Barcelona: Anthropos.

Sartre, Jean Paul
1940 *L'imaginaire. Psychologie phénoménologique de l'imagina-
      tion*, Paris: Gallimard.
1948 *Situations II*, Paris: Gallimard.

Sastre, Alfonso
1965 *Anatomía del realismo*, Barcelona: Seix Barral, 2nd edition, 1975.
1978 *Crítica de la imaginación*, Barcelona: Grijalbo.

Schaeffer, Susan Fromberg
1980 "The Unreality of Realism," *Critical Inquiry* 6, 4, pp. 727–737.

Schipper, Nineke
1979 *Realisme. De Illusie van werkelijkheid in literatur*, Assen and Brugge: Van Gorcum and Uitgeverijorion.

Schleusener, Jay
1980 "Convention and Context of Reading," *Critical Inquiry* 6, pp. 669–680.

Schmidt, Siegfried J.
1976 "Towards a Pragmatic Interpretation of 'Fictionality,'" in Teun A. van Dijk, *Pragmatics of Language*, pp. 161–178.
1978 "La ciencia de la literatura entre la lingüística y la sociopsicología (Algunos conceptos y problemas teórico empíricos sobre una ciencia de la literatura)," *Dispositio* III, 7–88, pp. 39–70.
1979 "Empirische Literaturwissenschaft as Perspective," *Poetics* 8, pp. 557–568.
1980 "Receptional Problems with Contemporary Narrative/Texts and Some of their Reasons," *Poetics* 9, pp. 119–146.
1980b "Fictionality in Literary and Non-Literary Discourse," *Poetics* 9, pp. 525–546.
1980c *Grundriss der Empirischen Literaturwissenschaft. Vol 1. Der gesellschaftliche Handlungsbereich Literatur*, Braunschweig-Wiesbaden: Wieweg und Sohn. English edition: *Foundations for the Empirical Study of Literature. The Components of a Basic Theory*, trans. by Robert de Beaugrande, Hamburg: Helmut Buske Verlag, 1982.
1981 "Empirical Studies in Literature: Introductory Remarks," *Poetics* 10, pp. 317–336.
1984 "The Fiction is That Reality Exists. A Constructivist Model of Reality, Fiction, and Literature," *Poetics Today* 5, 2, pp. 253–274.

Schor, Naomi
1984 "Details and Realism: *Le curé de Tours*," *Poetics Today* 5, 4, pp. 701–709.

Schultz, Robert A.
1979 "Analogues of Argument in Fictional Narrative," *Poetics* 8, 1979, pp. 231–244.

Schwartz, Elias
1972 *The Forms of Feeling: Toward a Mimetic Theory of Literature*, Port Washington: Kennikat Press.

Searle, John
1969 *Speech Acts. An Essay in the Philosophy of Language*, Cambridge: Cambridge University Press.
1975 "The Logical Status of Fictional Discourse," *New Literary History* 2, pp. 319–332.
1980 "Las Meninas and the Paradoxes of Pictorial Representation," *Critical Inquiry* 6, 3, pp. 477–488.
1983 *Intentionality. An Essay in the Philosophy of Mind*, Cambridge: Cambridge University Press.

Segre, Cesare
1978 "Divagazioni su mimesi e menzogna," in Lea Ritter Santini and Ezio Raimondi (editors), *Retorica e critica letteraria*, Bologna: Il Mulino, pp. 179–185.
1985 *Principios de análisis del texto literario*, Barcelona: Crítica.

Senabre, Ricardo
1987 *Literatura y público*, Madrid: Paraninfo.

Slama-Cazacu, Tatiana
1970 *Lenguaje y contexto*. Spanish translation by Carla del Solar, Barcelona-México: Grijalbo.

Smith, Barbara H.
1970 "Literature as Performance, Fiction and Art," *The Journal of Philosophy* 67, 16, pp. 553–563.
1971 "Poetry as Fiction," *New Literary History* II, 2, pp. 259–281.
1978 *On the Margins of Discourse*, Chicago and London: The University of Chicago Press.
1980 "Narrative Versions, Narrative Theories," *Critical Inquiry* 7, 1, pp. 213–236.

Sörbom, Göran
1966 *Mimesis and Art: Studies in the Origin and Early Development of an Aesthetic Vocabulary*, Uppsala: Svenska Bokforlaget Bonniers.

Souché-Dagues, D.
1972 *Le développement de l'intentionalité dans la phénoménologie husserlienne*, The Hague: M. Nijhoff.

Spariosu, Mihai I.
1982 *Literature, Mimesis and Play: Essays in Literary Theory*, Tübingen: Gunter Narr Verlag.

Spariosu, Mihai I. (editor)
1984 *Mimesis in Contemporary Theory: An Interdisciplinary Approach*. Vol. 1: *The Literary and Philosophical Debate*, Philadelphia and Amsterdam: John Benjamins Publ.

Stern, J. P.
1973 *On Realism*, London and Boston: Routledge & Kegan Paul.

Stierle, Karlheinz
1975 "Réception et fiction," *Poétique* 39, pp. 299–320.

Stout, Jeffrey
1982 "What is the Meaning of a Text?," *New Literary History* 1, pp. 1–12.

Styan, J. L.
1981 *Modern Drama in Theory and Practice. 1. Realism and Naturalism*, Cambridge: Cambridge University Press.

Suleiman, Susan R., and Crossman, Inge (editors)
1980 *The Reader in the Text. Essays on Audience and Interpretation*, Princeton: Princeton University Press.

Taléns, Jenaro
1986 "El análisis textual: Estrategias discursivas y producción de sentido," *Eutopías* 2, 1, pp. 9–26.

Taléns, Jenaro, and Company, J. M.
1984 "The Textual Space. On the Notion of the Text," *MMLA* 17, 2, pp. 24–36.
1985 "De la retórica como ideología," *Eutopías* 1, 3, pp. 203–230.

Tallis, Raymond
1988 *In Defence of Realism*, London: Edward Arnold.

Tarrío, Ángel
1976 "Presupuestos para una semiología del realismo en literatura," *Linguistica e Letteratura* 1, 2, pp. 49–79.
1979 "Las competencias del lector realista," *Senara* 1, pp. 209–228.

Tarski, Alfred
1944 "The Semantic Conception of Truth and the Foundations of Semantics," *Philosophy and Phenomenological Research* IV, pp. 341–375.

Tatarkiewicz, Wladyslaw
1987 "Mimesis: historia de la relación del arte con la realidad," in *Historia de seis ideas*, Madrid: Tecnos, pp. 301–324.

Tate, J.
1928 "'Imitation'" in Plato's *Republic*," *Classical Quarterly* XXII, pp. 16–23.
1932 "Plato and 'Imitation'," *Classical Quarterly* XXVI, pp. 161–169.

Teige, Karel
1982 *Surrealismo, realismo socialista, irrealismo. 1934–1951*, Torino: Einaudi.

Tieje, A. J.
1913 "A Peculiar Phase of the Theory of Realism in PreRichardsonian Prose-Fiction," *PMLA* XXVII, pp. 213–252.

Todorov, Tzvetan
1968 "Du vraisemblable que l'on ne saurait éviter," *Communications* 11, pp. 145–147.
1970 *Introduction à la littérature fantastique*, Paris: Seuil.
1971 *Poétique de la prose*, Paris: Seuil.
1975 "La lecture comme construction," *Poétique* 24, pp. 417–425.
1977 *Théories du symbole*, Paris: Seuil.
1978 *Les genres du discours*, Paris: Seuil.

Tompkins, Jane P.
1980 *Reader-Response Criticism. From Formalism to Poststructuralism*, Baltimore and London: The Johns Hopkins University Press.

Trench, W. F.
1933 "Mimesis in Aristotle's *Poetics*," *Hermathena*, 48, pp. 1–24.

Tyminiecka, Anna-Teresa
1983 "The Phenomenological Conception of the Possible World and the Creative Function of Man," *Analecta Husserliana* 14, pp. 353–373.

Urban, Wilbur Marshall
1939 *Language and Reality: The Philosophy of Language and the Principles of Symbolism*, London: George Allen & Unwin.

Vaihinger, Hans
1911 *Die Philosophie des Als-Ob*. English edition: *The Philosophy of As If*, trans. by C. K. Ogden, London: Routledege & Kegan Paul, 1924. 1968.

Valesio, Paolo
1974 "On Reality and Unreality in Language," *Semiotica* X, 1, pp. 75–91.

Various Authors
1967 "Realism: A Symposium," *Monatshefte für Deutschen Unterricht*, pp. 97–130.
1973 "Le discours réaliste," *Poétique* 16.
1974 *Le réel et le texte*, Paris: Armand Colin.
1975 *Brecht y el realismo dialéctico*, ed. by Juan Antonio Hormigón, Madrid: Comunicación.
1980 "Le détail et son inconscient," *Littérature* 37.
1984 "The Construction of Reality in Fiction,"*Poetics Today* 5, 2.

Vax, Louis
1965 *La séduction de l'étrange. Etude sur la littérature fantastique*, Paris: P. U. F.
1979 *Les chefs d'oeuvre de la littérature fantastique*, Paris: P. U. F.

Vázquez, Juan
1986 *Lenguaje, verdad y mundo. Modelo fenomenológico de análisis semántico*, Barcelona: Anthropos.

Verdenius, W. J.
1949 *Mimesis: Plato's Doctrine of Artistic Imitation and Its Meaning to Us*, Leiden: E. J. Brill.

Vernois, Paul (editor)
1967 *Le réel dans la littérature et dans la langue: Actes du Xe Congrès de la Fédération internationale des langues et littératures modernes*, Paris: Klincksieck.

Villanueva, Darío
1984 "Narratario y lectores implícitos en la evolución formal de la novela picaresca," in Luis González del Valle and D. Villanueva (editors), *Estudios en honor a Ricardo Gullón*, Lincoln: Society of Spanish and Spanish American Studies, pp. 343–367.

Waldman, Marilyn Robinson
1981 "'The Otherwise Unnoteworthy Year 711': A Reply to Hayden White," *Critical Inquiry* 7, 4, pp. 784–792.

Walton, Kendall
1978 "How Remote Are Fictional Worlds from the Real World?" *The Journal of Aesthetics and Art Criticism* 388, pp. 11–23.
1980 "Appreciating Fiction: Suspending Disbelief or Pretending Belief," *Dispositio* V, 13–14, pp. 1–18.
1984 "Transparent Pictures: On the Nature of Photographic Realism," *Critical Inquiry* 11, pp. 246–277.

Warning, Rainer
1979 "Pour une pragmatique du discours fictionnel," *Poétique* 39, pp. 321–337.

Watt, Ian
1957 *The Rise of the Novel. Studies in Defoe, Richardson and Fielding*, London: Chatto & Windus.

Watzlawick, Paul (editor)
1984 *The Invented Reality: How Do We Know What We Believe We Know? Contributions to Constructivism*, New York: Norton.

Weinberg, Bernard
1937 *French Realism: The Critical Reaction, 1830–1870*, reprinted, New York: Krauss, 1971.

Wellek, René
1942 "The Mode of Existence of a Literary Work of Art," *Southern Review* 7, pp. 735–754.
1954 "Auerbach's Special Realism," *Kenyon Review* 16, pp. 299–307.
1961 "The Concept of Realism in Literary Scholarship," *Neophilologus* 45, pp. 1–20.
1962 "A Reply to E. B. Greenwood's Reflections," *Neophilologus* 46, pp. 194–196.
1982 "Literature, Fiction, and Literariness," *The Attack on Literature*, Brighton: The Harvester Press, pp. 19–32.

White, Hayden
1980 "The Value of Narrativity in the Representation of Reality," *Critical Inquiry* 7, 1, pp. 5–27.
1981 "The Narrativization of Real Events," *Critical Inquiry*, pp. 793–798.
1987 *The Content of Form. Narrative Discourse and Historical Representation*, Baltimore and London: The Johns Hopkins University Press, 2nd edition, 1989.

Whorf, Lee B.
1956 *Language, Thought, and Reality*, Cambridge: The M.I.T. Press.

Wienold, Götz
1973 "Experimental Research on Literature: Its Need and Appropriateness," *Poetics* 7, pp. 77–85.

Wildekamp, Ada I. van Montfort, and van Ruiswyk, W.
1980 "Fictionality and Convention," *Poetics* 9, pp. 547–567.

Wimsatt, W. K.
1954 *The Verbal Icon*, London: Methuen & Co.
1968 "Genesis. A Fallacy Revisited," in Peter Demetz and others, *The Disciplines of Criticism: Essays in Literary Theory, Interpretation, and History*, New Haven: Yale University Press, pp. 193–225.
1975 "In Search of Verbal Mimesis," *Yale French Studies* 52, pp. 229–248.

Wittgenstein, Ludwig
1921 *Tractatus Logico-Philosophicus*, trans. by C. K. Ogden, introduction by Bertrand Russell, London: Routledge and Kegan Paul, 1981.
1958 *Philosophical Investigations*, trans. by G. E. M. Anscombe, Oxford: Blackwell.

Wolterstorff, Nicholas
1979 "Characters and their Names," *Poetics* 8, pp. 101–127.
1980 *Works and Worlds of Art*, Oxford: Clarendon Press.

Woods, John Hayden
1974 *The Logic of Fiction. A Philosophical Sounding of Deviant Logic*, The Hague and Paris: Mouton.

Woods, John, and Pavel, Thomas G. (editors)
1979 *Formal Semantics and Literary Theory*, Poetics 88, 1/2. "Introduction," pp. 1–2.

Wundt, Max
1930 "La ciencia literaria y la teoría de la concepción del mundo," in Emil Ermatinger (editor), *Filosofía de la ciencia literaria*, Mexico: F. C. E., 1946, 2nd edition 1984, pp. 427–452.

Zabarzadeh, Mas'ud
1977 *The Mythopoeic Reality: The Postwar American Nonfiction Novel*, Urbana: University of Illinois Press.

Zgorzelski, Andrezej
1984 "On Differentiating Fantastic Fiction: Some Supragenological Distinctions in Literature," *Poetics Today* 5, 2, pp. 299–307.

Zilliacus, Clas
1979 "Radical Naturalism: First-Person Documentary Literature," *Comparative Literature* 31, 2, pp. 97–112.

Zola, Emile
1971 *Le roman expérimental*, chronology and preface by Aime
     Gueds, Paris: Garnier-Flammarion.

Zubiri, Xavier
1989 *Estructura dinámica de la realidad*, Madrid: Alianza Editorial.

INDEX OF NAMES